Coin Collecting | [10 in 1]

From Beginner to Expert | Master Complete Guide to Identifying, Valuing, and Preserving Coins, Uncovering Rare Finds, and Avoiding Scams

Sylvester K. Abbott

Copyright © 2024 by Sylvester K. Abbott

Disclaimer Notice

Thank You For Reading!

I hope you will enjoy reading it as much as I enjoyed writing it.

Your support means so much to me!

If you find value in these pages, I kindly ask you to consider supporting me with your feedback.

Your feedback not only helps me improve but also helps other readers discover this book.

YOUR GIFTS ARE WAITING FOR YOU!

To enhance your experience and to give you additional help, I have prepared some great bonuses for you!

Find download instructions at the end of the book.

I'm confident you'll love these additional resources!

Table of Contents

Introduction

Welcome to the fascinating realm of numismatics, where every coin tells a story—of empires risen and fallen, of cultural exchange and economic evolution, and of the passions that drive collectors across the globe. In this comprehensive guide, we embark on a journey through centuries of human history, exploring the art, science, and thrill of coin collecting.

Numismatics is more than a hobby; it is a vibrant intersection of art, history, and economics. Through the study of coins, we gain insights into the societies that minted them—their beliefs, achievements, and struggles. From the ancient coins of Greece bearing the likenesses of gods and goddesses to the modern currencies reflecting the spirit of nations, each piece is a tangible link to our collective past.

This book is your passport to understanding and mastering the world of coin collecting. Whether you are a novice eager to start your collection or a seasoned collector seeking deeper knowledge, you will find here a wealth of information. We will delve into the intricacies of coin grading, explore the nuances of valuation, and uncover the secrets of detecting counterfeits. You will discover the joy of assembling thematic collections, the thrill of uncovering rare specimens, and the satisfaction of preserving history in your hands.

Join us as we explore the artistry of coin design, the technology behind minting, and the cultural significance embedded in each coin. Learn about the ethical considerations that guide responsible collecting and gain insights into the future trends shaping the hobby. With each turn of the page, you will uncover new perspectives and find inspiration to expand your horizons in the vibrant world of numismatics.

Whether your interest lies in ancient coins that whisper tales of forgotten civilizations or in modern treasures that reflect the pulse of contemporary society, this book aims to be your trusted companion—a comprehensive guide, a source of inspiration, and a celebration of the enduring allure of coins.

Welcome to the journey of discovery. Welcome to the world of numismatics.

BOOK 1

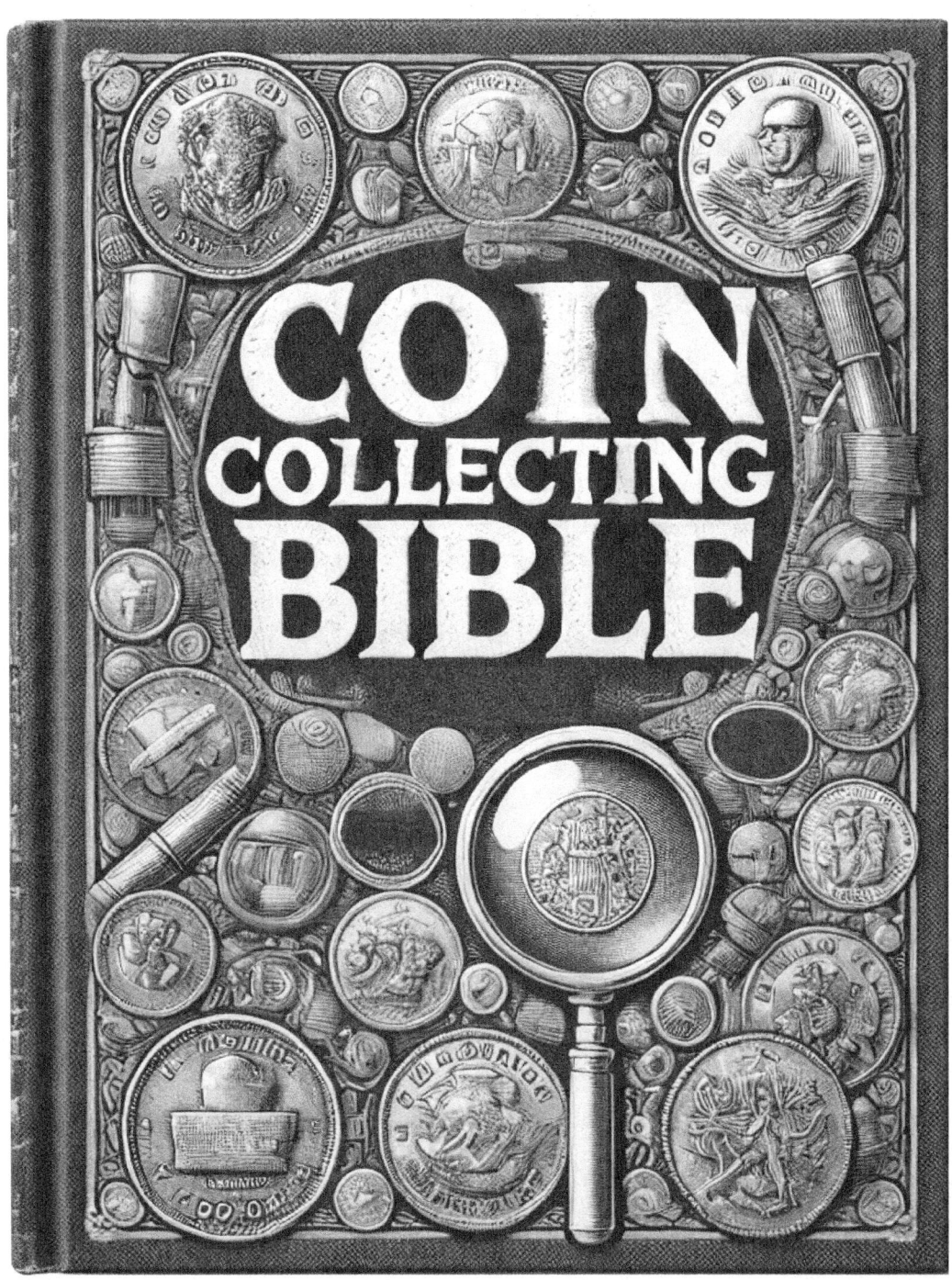

Chapter 1: Introduction to Numismatics

Numismatics, derived from the Greek word "nomisma" meaning coin, is the scholarly study and collection of coins, tokens, paper money, and related objects. It encompasses a broad spectrum of interests, ranging from the historical, cultural, and artistic aspects of coins to their economic and technological significance.

At its core, numismatics seeks to understand the role of currency in human history and civilization. Coins are not merely objects of monetary exchange; they are tangible artifacts that encapsulate the political, social, and economic landscapes of their time. They bear witness to the rise and fall of empires, the triumphs of rulers, and the aspirations of societies.

Beyond their monetary value, coins serve as windows into the past, offering glimpses into the artistic styles, religious beliefs, and technological advancements of ancient and modern cultures alike. They provide crucial evidence for historians and archaeologists, shedding light on trade routes, political alliances, and cultural interactions.

Numismatists study coins through various lenses: from deciphering inscriptions and symbols to evaluating their condition and rarity. They classify coins by historical period, geographic region, and minting authority, creating comprehensive catalogs that serve as invaluable references for collectors and scholars alike.

In essence, numismatics bridges disciplines—art history, archaeology, economics, and sociology—offering a multidimensional perspective on human civilization. It invites enthusiasts to explore the beauty, diversity, and enduring legacy of coins while uncovering the stories embedded in each minted piece.

As we embark on this journey through the world of numismatics, we invite you to delve deeper into the intricate tapestry of coins—their past, their present significance, and their enduring fascination.

Chapter 2: Brief History of Coinage: From Barter to Global Currency

Coins, as we know them today, are the culmination of millennia of human ingenuity and necessity. The evolution of coinage parallels the development of human civilization itself, marking significant milestones in trade, economics, and cultural exchange.

1. Origins of Money and Early Forms of Currency:

- **Barter and Commodity Money:** Before coins, societies engaged in barter, trading goods and services directly. However, barter had limitations—unequal value of goods, perishability, and indivisibility.

- **Commodity Money:** To address these challenges, societies began using commodities with intrinsic value—such as shells, cattle, grain, and metals—as mediums of exchange. These early forms of money laid the foundation for the concept of standardized value in transactions.

2. The Emergence of Metal Coinage:

- **Ancient Near East:** The first true coins emerged in the late 7th century BCE in Lydia (modern-day Turkey), made of electrum (a natural alloy of gold and silver). These coins featured a stamp to guarantee their weight and purity, facilitating trade beyond local boundaries.

- **Greek and Roman Coinage:** The Greeks and later the Romans standardized coinage, using various metals—gold, silver, and bronze—marked with images of rulers, gods, and symbols of their respective cultures. Roman coins, in particular, spread throughout their vast empire, becoming symbols of imperial power and unity.

3. Medieval and Early Modern Coinage:

- **Islamic Coinage:** The Islamic world introduced significant advancements in coin design and minting techniques, with intricate calligraphy and geometric patterns.

- **European Renaissance:** The Renaissance saw a revival of coinage in Europe, with new designs reflecting cultural and artistic movements. Sovereigns and monarchs used coins to promote their authority and project national identity.

4. The Age of Exploration and Global Trade:

- **Colonial Coinage:** European exploration and colonization led to the global spread of coinage. Colonial powers minted coins for trade and control, influencing local economies and cultures.

- **Global Trade Networks:** The rise of global trade networks in the 16th to 19th centuries further standardized coinage, with currencies like the Spanish dollar (pieces of eight) becoming widely accepted internationally.

5. Modern Coinage and Fiat Currency:

- **Fiat Currency:** In the 20th century, most countries transitioned to fiat money—currency not backed by physical commodities but by the government's guarantee of its value. Coins continued to circulate alongside paper money, with designs reflecting national heritage and values.

6. Numismatics Today:

- **Collecting and Preservation:** Numismatics today encompasses the study and collection of coins for historical, artistic, and investment purposes. Collectors value coins for their rarity, condition, and cultural significance, contributing to a vibrant global community of enthusiasts.

The history of coinage is a testament to human innovation and creativity, reflecting our economic and cultural evolution over millennia. From humble beginnings as stamped pieces of metal to symbols of national identity and global trade, coins continue to play a crucial role in shaping our understanding of the past and present economic systems.

Chapter 3: The Importance of Coin Collecting

Coin collecting, also known as numismatics, holds significant value beyond the mere accumulation of currency. It encompasses historical, educational, artistic, and economic dimensions that enrich the lives of collectors and contribute to broader societal understanding. Here are some key aspects highlighting the importance of coin collecting:

1. Historical Insight:

- **Preservation of History:** Coins serve as tangible artifacts of historical periods, offering insights into the social, political, and economic conditions of their times. They are often the only surviving records of certain eras, particularly for ancient civilizations.

- **Chronicles of Rulers and Events:** Coins often feature portraits of rulers, commemorative events, and symbols of power, providing a chronological record of leadership and significant occurrences.

2. Educational Value:

- **Interdisciplinary Learning:** Coin collecting fosters a multidisciplinary approach to learning, incorporating history, geography, economics, and art. It encourages research and critical thinking.

- **Language and Symbolism:** Coins are rich in inscriptions and iconography, aiding in the study of ancient languages, alphabets, and symbolic representations.

3. Artistic Appreciation:

- **Numismatic Art:** Coins are miniature pieces of art, showcasing the craftsmanship of engravers and designers. They reflect the aesthetic values and artistic trends of their respective periods.

- **Cultural Expression:** The imagery and motifs on coins reveal cultural narratives and artistic styles, offering a window into the creative expressions of different societies.

4. Economic Significance:

- **Investment Potential:** Rare and historically significant coins can be valuable assets, appreciating over time. Collectors often view numismatics as a form of investment, diversifying their financial portfolios.

- **Market Dynamics:** The coin market, influenced by factors such as rarity, demand, and condition, provides insights into broader economic principles and trends.

5. Cultural and Heritage Preservation:

- **National Identity:** Coins often reflect national pride and heritage, featuring symbols, landmarks, and notable figures. They are tools for preserving and promoting cultural identity.

- **Community and Tradition:** Coin collecting fosters a sense of community among enthusiasts who share knowledge, stories, and a passion for history, contributing to the preservation of collective heritage.

6. Personal Fulfillment and Leisure:

- **Hobby and Passion:** For many, coin collecting is a fulfilling hobby that brings joy, relaxation, and a sense of achievement. It offers a rewarding way to spend leisure time, with the thrill of discovery and the satisfaction of building a collection.

- **Mental Stimulation:** The process of researching, cataloging, and organizing a coin collection stimulates the mind, enhancing cognitive skills and attention to detail.

7. Contributions to Scholarship and Research:

- **Academic Research:** Numismatists contribute to scholarly research by uncovering new historical evidence through coin finds. Their work helps to clarify historical narratives and correct misconceptions.

- **Publications and Exhibitions:** Collectors often share their knowledge through publications, articles, and exhibitions, making numismatic research accessible to a broader audience.

8. Societal Impact:

- **Economic Awareness:** Coin collecting raises awareness about economic history and the evolution of monetary systems, fostering a deeper understanding of contemporary economic issues.

- **Educational Programs:** Many museums and educational institutions use coins in their programs to teach history and economics, benefiting students and the general public.

In essence, coin collecting is a multifaceted pursuit that enriches individual lives and contributes to collective knowledge. It bridges past and present, blending the appreciation of art, history, and economics into a single, rewarding experience.

BOOK 2

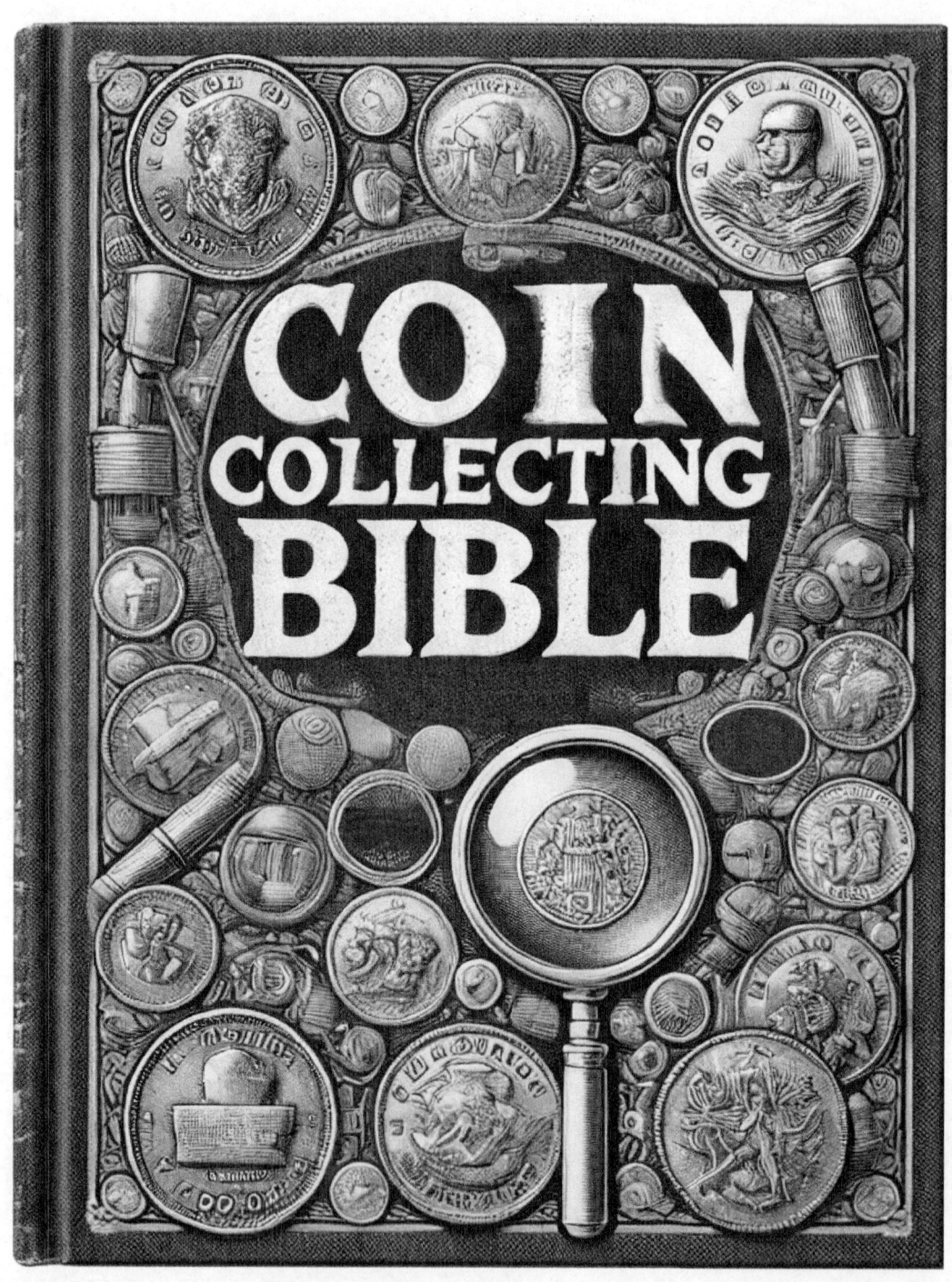

Chapter 1: Types of Coins

Coin collecting encompasses a wide variety of coins, each representing different periods, regions, and purposes. Here, we discuss several key categories of coins in detail: Ancient Coins, Medieval Coins, Modern Coins, Commemorative Coins, Bullion Coins, and Error Coins.

1. Ancient Coins

Greek Coins:

- **Archaic Period (circa 700-480 BCE):** Early Greek coins, made of electrum, featured simple designs like geometric patterns. Aegina's turtle coins and Athens' owl tetradrachms are notable examples.

- **Classical Period (circa 480-323 BCE):** More detailed, often depicting gods and goddesses, mythological scenes, and famous figures. The tetradrachm of Athens with Athena and the owl is iconic.

- **Hellenistic Period (circa 323-31 BCE):** Coins showed realistic portraits of rulers, influenced by Alexander the Great's conquests. The coins of the Ptolemies in Egypt and Seleucids in Asia are significant.

Roman Coins:

- **Republican Era (509-27 BCE):** Early Roman coins like the denarius featured symbols of the Republic and prominent historical figures.

- **Imperial Era (27 BCE-476 CE):** Coins prominently displayed emperors' portraits and propaganda messages. Julius Caesar's denarius and Constantine the Great's coins celebrating Christianity are examples.

- **Late Empire (3rd-5th centuries CE):** Debasement of coinage occurred, with emperors like Diocletian attempting reforms to stabilize currency.

Byzantine Coins:

- **Early Period (circa 4th-7th centuries CE):** Coins transitioned from Roman traditions, featuring Christian symbols and the solidus, a stable gold coin.

- **Middle Period (circa 7th-11th centuries CE):** Featured religious iconography, including Jesus Christ and the Virgin Mary. The miliaresion (silver) and follis (bronze) were common.

- **Late Period (circa 11th-15th centuries CE):** Continued focus on religious themes amidst economic decline, reflected in the quality of coinage.

2. Medieval Coins

European Coins:

- **Early Medieval (circa 5th-10th centuries CE):** Coins often imitated Roman and Byzantine designs. Notables are the Anglo-Saxon pennies and Frankish deniers.

- **High Medieval (circa 11th-15th centuries CE):** Coins began to reflect more local identities. Examples include English pennies, French deniers, and German pfennigs.

Islamic Coins:

- **Early Islamic Period:** Featured Arabic inscriptions and avoided imagery due to religious prohibitions. The dinar (gold) and dirham (silver) were significant.

- **Later Period:** Introduced intricate calligraphy and designs, influencing coinage across the Islamic world and beyond.

3. Modern Coins

Circulating Coins:

- **National Currencies:** Modern coins issued by sovereign states for everyday transactions, featuring national symbols, historical figures, and significant events.

- **Examples:** The U.S. quarter, the British pound coin, the euro coins, and the Japanese yen.

Specialized Collections:

- **Proof Sets and Mint Sets:** Specially minted for collectors, often with superior quality and packaging. Proof coins are struck with extra care to enhance detail.

- **Commemorative Coins:** Issued to celebrate significant events, anniversaries, or individuals, often in limited editions.

4. Commemorative Coins

Purpose:

- **Celebration and Memorialization:** These coins honor historical events, famous personalities, or cultural milestones. They are typically produced in limited quantities.

Examples:

- **U.S. Bicentennial Quarters (1976):** Marked the 200th anniversary of American independence.

- **Euro Commemorative Coins:** Issued by various Eurozone countries to celebrate diverse events, such as the anniversary of the Treaty of Rome.

5. Bullion Coins

Investment Purpose:

- **Precious Metal Content:** Bullion coins are valued for their precious metal content (gold, silver, platinum) rather than their face value. They are popular among investors as a hedge against inflation.

Examples:

- **American Gold Eagle:** A popular gold bullion coin issued by the United States.

- **Canadian Silver Maple Leaf:** Known for its high silver content and purity.

6. Error Coins

Significance:

- **Minting Mistakes:** Error coins result from mistakes during the minting process, making them rare and often valuable to collectors.

Types:

- **Die Errors:** Misalignment or cracks in the die can create double strikes or off-center images.

- **Planchet Errors:** Mistakes in the blank metal discs used for coins, leading to incorrect shapes or compositions.

- **Striking Errors:** Issues during the actual striking process, such as overstrikes or weak strikes.

Examples:

- **1955 Doubled Die Lincoln Cent:** A famous U.S. coin with a noticeable doubling of the date and inscriptions.

- **2000 Sacagawea Dollar/Washington Quarter Mule:** A U.S. coin featuring a mismatched obverse and reverse.

Chapter 2: Significance of Different Types of Coins

Each type of coin offers unique insights into various aspects of human civilization, from ancient societies to modern economies. Collectors and scholars value these coins not only for their monetary worth but also for their historical, artistic, and cultural significance. Studying different types of coins provides a comprehensive understanding of the diverse narratives that have shaped our world.

Special Collections and Sets

Special collections and sets are prized in the world of numismatics for their uniqueness, historical significance, artistic beauty, and investment potential. These collections, often meticulously curated, offer collectors a deeper appreciation of the craft and history of coin minting. Here, we delve into various categories of special collections and sets, exploring their features, significance, and examples.

1. Proof Sets

Definition:

- Proof sets are collections of coins that have been struck using specially prepared dies and planchets, resulting in coins of exceptional quality with mirror-like finishes and sharp details.

Features:

- **Striking Process:** Proof coins are struck multiple times with polished dies to enhance details and achieve a high-quality finish.

- **Finish:** They typically feature a mirror-like background with frosted designs, creating a contrast that highlights the coin's artwork.

- **Packaging:** Proof sets are often housed in protective cases to prevent damage and preserve their condition, making them ideal for display.

Examples:

- **United States Proof Sets:** These annual sets include proof versions of all circulating U.S. coins for that year, from pennies to dollars. They often come in attractive packaging with certificates of authenticity.

- **Royal Mint Proof Sets:** Issued by the UK's Royal Mint, these sets feature proof versions of British coins and are popular among collectors for their quality and design.

2. Mint Sets

Definition:

- Mint sets, also known as uncirculated sets, contain coins struck with regular dies but selected for their superior quality. These coins have not been circulated and retain their mint condition.

Features:

- **Condition:** Uncirculated coins with no wear and tear, exhibiting sharper details and cleaner surfaces than circulated coins.

- **Packaging:** Typically housed in special packaging to identify them as mint sets and protect them from handling damage.

Examples:

- **United States Mint Sets:** These include uncirculated versions of all U.S. coins issued in a particular year, providing collectors with high-quality examples of everyday coinage.

- **Canadian Mint Sets:** Issued by the Royal Canadian Mint, these sets feature uncirculated versions of Canadian coins, often including special editions or commemoratives.

3. Commemorative Coin Sets

Definition:

- Commemorative coin sets are issued to mark significant events, anniversaries, or milestones. These sets often include coins with special designs that are not part of regular circulation.

Features:

- **Themes:** Coins in these sets celebrate historical events, cultural milestones, notable personalities, or national achievements.

- **Limited Editions:** Produced in limited quantities, increasing their rarity and desirability among collectors.

- **Special Designs:** Unique artwork and inscriptions relevant to the occasion being commemorated, often with high artistic value.

Examples:

- **U.S. Bicentennial Coin Set (1976):** Issued to celebrate the 200th anniversary of American independence, including special designs for the quarter, half dollar, and dollar.

- **Royal Mint Commemorative Sets:** Feature coins celebrating events such as royal anniversaries, significant historical milestones, and cultural icons.

4. Thematic Collections

Definition:

- Thematic collections are sets of coins assembled based on a specific theme, such as wildlife, space exploration, famous personalities, or historical periods.

Features:

- **Consistency:** Coins in the set share a common theme, creating a cohesive and interesting collection.

- **Educational Value:** These sets often provide insights into the theme, offering both aesthetic enjoyment and educational content.

Examples:

- **Wildlife Series:** Coins featuring various animals, such as the Canadian Wildlife Series, showcasing Canadian fauna on high-quality silver coins.

- **Historical Figures:** Sets depicting influential historical figures, such as the U.S. Presidential Dollar Series, which honors past presidents of the United States.

5. Bullion Coin Sets

Definition:

- Bullion coin sets consist of coins made from precious metals like gold, silver, platinum, or palladium, valued primarily for their metal content.

Features:

- **Investment Value:** These sets are often purchased for their precious metal value as well as their collectible appeal.

- **Purity and Weight:** Coins are typically marked with their weight and metal purity, making them a reliable store of value.

Examples:

- **American Eagle Bullion Sets:** Include gold, silver, and platinum coins issued by the United States Mint, known for their high purity and iconic designs.

- **Canadian Maple Leaf Bullion Sets:** Feature gold, silver, and platinum coins recognized worldwide for their purity and quality.

6. Error Coin Sets

Definition:

- Error coin sets consist of coins that contain minting mistakes, such as misprints, off-center strikes, or planchet errors.

Features:

- **Rarity:** Errors are generally rare, making these sets highly sought after by collectors.

- **Variety:** Errors can occur in many forms, offering a diverse and intriguing collection.

Types of Errors:

- **Die Errors:** Misalignment or cracks in the die can create double strikes or off-center images.

- **Planchet Errors:** Mistakes in the blank metal discs used for coins, leading to incorrect shapes or compositions.

- **Striking Errors:** Issues during the actual striking process, such as overstrikes or weak strikes.

Examples:

- **1955 Doubled Die Lincoln Cent:** A famous U.S. coin with a noticeable doubling of the date and inscriptions.

- **2000 Sacagawea Dollar/Washington Quarter Mule:** A U.S. coin featuring a mismatched obverse and reverse.

Significance of Special Collections and Sets

Enhancement of Collection:

- Special collections and sets add depth and variety to a coin collection, offering collectors unique and high-quality pieces that stand out.

Educational and Historical Value:

- These sets often commemorate significant events or themes, making them not only valuable but also educational, enriching the collector's understanding of history and culture.

Investment Potential:

- Limited edition sets and high-quality proof coins can appreciate in value over time, providing both aesthetic pleasure and financial benefit.

Community and Tradition:

- Collecting special sets fosters a sense of community among enthusiasts who share similar interests and passion, promoting the tradition of numismatics.

Special collections and sets represent the pinnacle of coin collecting, combining artistry, history, and rarity. They offer a rewarding experience for collectors, providing both intellectual enrichment and potential financial gain. Whether celebrating significant historical events, showcasing artistic excellence, or preserving numismatic errors, these collections enhance the appreciation of the diverse and fascinating world of coins.

Chapter 3: Fakes and Forgeries: Common Types of Counterfeit Coins

The world of coin collecting is not immune to the presence of fakes and forgeries. Counterfeit coins can deceive even experienced collectors, making it essential to understand the common types and how to identify them. Here, we explore the most prevalent types of counterfeit coins, their characteristics, and some tips for detection.

1. Cast Counterfeits

Description:

- Cast counterfeits are made by creating molds from genuine coins and then casting new coins using molten metal.

Characteristics:

- **Surface Texture:** Often have a rough or granular surface due to the casting process.

- **Details:** Tend to lack the sharpness and fine details of genuine coins, as the casting process cannot perfectly replicate the original.

- **Weight and Sound:** May differ slightly in weight and produce a different sound when dropped compared to genuine coins.

Detection Tips:

- **Magnification:** Use a magnifying glass or microscope to inspect the surface texture and details.

- **Weight Check:** Use a precise scale to compare the weight with known standards for the coin type.

- **Sound Test:** Gently drop the coin and listen to the sound; genuine coins typically have a distinct ring, while cast counterfeits may sound dull.

2. Electrotype Counterfeits

Description:

- Electrotype counterfeits are made by electroplating a base metal with a thin layer of the desired metal, usually replicating both sides of the coin separately and then joining them together.

Characteristics:

- **Seam Line:** Often have a visible seam line around the edge where the two halves are joined.

- **Surface:** The surface may show signs of electroplating, such as uneven color or texture.

- **Weight and Composition:** The core metal may differ from the original, affecting the coin's weight and magnetic properties.

Detection Tips:

- **Edge Inspection:** Look for a seam line around the coin's edge using a magnifying glass.

- **Magnet Test:** Test the coin with a magnet; genuine coins of certain metals are non-magnetic, whereas electrotypes with base metal cores may be magnetic.

- **Density Test:** Measure the coin's density by calculating its volume and comparing it with the known density of the genuine coin's metal.

3. Struck Counterfeits

Description:

- Struck counterfeits are made using dies to strike metal blanks, similar to the process used for genuine coins, but using unauthorized or counterfeit dies.

Characteristics:

- **Die Flaws:** May show repeated die flaws or inconsistencies in the design due to the use of inferior or mismatched dies.

- **Metal Quality:** Often made from lower-quality metal that does not match the composition of genuine coins.

- **Details:** While they can have sharp details, there may be subtle differences in the design elements or lettering.

Detection Tips:

- **Comparison:** Compare the suspected counterfeit with a genuine coin under magnification, paying close attention to design details and lettering.

- **Metal Analysis:** Conduct a metal composition analysis using X-ray fluorescence (XRF) or other methods to check for authenticity.

- **Authentication Services:** Utilize professional authentication and grading services for an expert opinion.

4. Altered Coins

Description:

- Altered coins are genuine coins that have been modified to appear as more valuable versions, such as by altering the date or mint mark.

Characteristics:

- **Date and Mint Mark Alterations:** Look for inconsistencies or signs of tampering around the date or mint mark area.

- **Surface Marks:** There may be tool marks or signs of re-engraving on the coin's surface.

- **Unnatural Wear:** The wear on the altered part may not match the overall wear of the coin.

Detection Tips:

- **Magnification:** Examine the date and mint mark area closely under magnification for signs of tampering.

- **Historical Knowledge:** Know the characteristics of genuine coins for the specific date and mint mark to spot discrepancies.

- **Professional Opinion:** Seek an expert's opinion if you suspect a coin has been altered.

5. Contemporary Counterfeits

Description:

- Contemporary counterfeits are coins that were produced at the same time as genuine coins but were intended to circulate as money rather than deceive collectors.

Characteristics:

- **Crude Appearance:** Often have a cruder appearance compared to genuine coins, as they were made with less sophisticated technology.

- **Materials:** May be made from base metals rather than the precious metals used in genuine coins.

- **Circulation Wear:** Often show signs of wear consistent with circulation.

Detection Tips:

- **Historical Context:** Understand the historical context and economic conditions that led to the production of contemporary counterfeits.

- **Material Analysis:** Check the coin's composition to see if it matches that of genuine coins from the period.

- **Expert Consultation:** Consult with experts who specialize in the period and type of coins you are collecting.

Counterfeit coins are a significant concern in numismatics, but understanding the common types and characteristics of these fakes can help collectors protect themselves. Always conduct thorough examinations, use reliable reference materials, and consider professional authentication services when in doubt. Being vigilant and knowledgeable is the best defense against acquiring counterfeit coins.

Techniques for Identifying Fake Coins

Identifying fake coins requires a combination of keen observation, knowledge, and the use of specialized tools and techniques. Here, we explore several effective methods to help collectors and numismatists detect counterfeit coins and protect their collections.

1. Visual Inspection

Magnification:

- **Use a Magnifying Glass or Microscope:** Inspect the coin under high magnification to examine fine details. Look for inconsistencies in the design, lettering, and surface texture.

- **Surface Quality:** Genuine coins have sharp details and consistent surface textures. Counterfeits often show signs of casting, such as pitting or rough surfaces.

Design and Lettering:

- **Compare with Known Genuine Coins:** Use reference materials or genuine coins for comparison. Pay attention to the size, shape, and alignment of design elements and lettering.

- **Look for Errors and Irregularities:** Check for misspelled words, incorrect fonts, or design elements that don't match genuine examples.

Edge Examination:

- **Check the Edge for Seams:** Electrotype counterfeits may have visible seams around the edge where two halves were joined.

- **Inspect for Reeding or Edge Inscriptions:** Genuine coins often have reeding (ridges) or inscriptions on the edge that are difficult to replicate perfectly.

2. Weight and Dimensions

Precise Measurement:

- **Use a Digital Scale:** Weigh the coin and compare its weight to the standard weight for that type of coin. Counterfeits often have weight discrepancies due to different metal compositions.

- **Measure Diameter and Thickness:** Use calipers to measure the coin's diameter and thickness. Deviations from standard dimensions can indicate a counterfeit.

Specific Gravity Test:

- **Calculate Density:** Measure the coin's volume by water displacement and calculate its density. Compare the result with the known density of the metal the coin is supposed to be made of. Counterfeit coins often use less dense metals.

3. Sound Test

Ping Test:

- **Conduct a Ring Test:** Gently tap the coin with a metal object and listen to the sound it produces. Genuine coins often have a distinct, clear ring, while counterfeits may produce a duller sound due to different metal compositions.

4. Magnet Test

Magnetic Properties:

- **Check with a Magnet:** Test the coin with a strong magnet. Genuine coins made from non-magnetic metals like gold, silver, or certain alloys will not be attracted to the magnet. Counterfeit coins made with magnetic core metals may be attracted.

5. Metal Composition Analysis

X-ray Fluorescence (XRF):

- **Conduct a Non-destructive Test:** Use XRF analyzers to determine the metal composition of the coin. This technology can identify the elements present in the coin without damaging it, revealing discrepancies in alloy content.

Acid Test:

- **Testing Precious Metals:** For coins made of gold or silver, an acid test can help verify their authenticity. Apply a small drop of acid to the coin and observe the reaction. However, this method can damage the coin, so it should be used with caution and preferably on less valuable specimens.

6. Die Analysis

Die Characteristics:

- **Study Die Marks:** Examine the coin for specific die marks and characteristics that are unique to genuine coins, such as die cracks, polish lines, and other minor imperfections.

- **Look for Repeated Flaws:** Counterfeit coins made from the same die may show repeated flaws or anomalies that are not present in genuine coins.

7. Authentication and Certification

Professional Services:

- **Third-party Grading Services:** Submit the coin to a reputable third-party grading service, such as the Professional Coin Grading Service (PCGS) or the Numismatic Guaranty Corporation (NGC). These organizations provide expert authentication, grading, and encapsulation, adding a layer of protection and assurance.

Expert Consultation:

- **Seek Advice from Experts:** Consult with experienced numismatists or coin dealers who specialize in the type of coin you are examining. Their expertise and knowledge can be invaluable in identifying fakes.

8. Historical Research

Provenance and Documentation:

- **Trace the Coin's History:** Verify the provenance of the coin. Documentation and previous ownership records can provide clues about its authenticity.

- **Market Knowledge:** Stay informed about common counterfeits and the history of counterfeit production for specific types of coins. Knowledge of common counterfeiting techniques and trends can aid in detection.

Identifying fake coins requires a combination of observational skills, specialized tools, and knowledge of numismatics. By using these techniques, collectors can better protect themselves from counterfeit coins and ensure the authenticity of their collections. Regularly educating oneself on new counterfeiting methods and consulting with experts are also crucial steps in maintaining a high-quality and genuine coin collection.

Case Studies of Famous Coin Forgeries

The history of coin collecting is dotted with instances of remarkable forgeries that have deceived collectors, experts, and even institutions. These case studies provide insights into the ingenuity of counterfeiters and the importance of vigilance and expertise in numismatics.

1. The 1933 Saint-Gaudens Double Eagle

Background:

- The 1933 Saint-Gaudens Double Eagle is one of the most famous and valuable U.S. coins. Although 445,500 were minted, they were never officially released due to President Franklin D. Roosevelt's executive order banning gold ownership to help stabilize the economy during the Great Depression.

Forgery Case:

- In 1944, a few examples surfaced, allegedly stolen from the U.S. Mint. Despite efforts to retrieve them, several escaped into the market. One such coin was famously auctioned in 2002 for $7.59 million after being seized by the Secret Service and then sold by the U.S. Mint under unique circumstances.

Detection and Outcome:

- The coin was authenticated through a combination of historical research, expert analysis, and provenance tracing. The case highlights the importance of thorough documentation and legal aspects in numismatic forgeries.

2. The Omega Man Counterfeits

Background:

- In the early 1970s, a mysterious counterfeiter known as the "Omega Man" produced high-quality forgeries of gold coins, including the $20 Saint-Gaudens Double Eagle and the $3 Indian Head gold coin.

Forgery Case:

- The counterfeits were almost indistinguishable from genuine coins, but they contained a hidden "Omega" symbol within the design, often in the folds of Liberty's gown or the eagle's feathers.

Detection and Outcome:

- Experts eventually identified the Omega symbol using magnification and careful examination. These coins now have collector interest due to their high-quality forgery and the mystery surrounding their creator.

3. The Black Cabinet 1794 Flowing Hair Dollar

Background:

- The 1794 Flowing Hair Silver Dollar is a highly coveted coin, believed to be one of the first silver dollars minted by the United States. Genuine examples are extremely rare and valuable.

Forgery Case:

- In the 1950s, a counterfeit example emerged, known as the "Black Cabinet" forgery, named after the collection it was part of. This coin was made using genuine U.S. Mint dies but struck illegally outside the mint.

Detection and Outcome:

- The coin's authenticity was questioned due to its unusual surface and weight. Detailed metallurgical analysis and comparisons with known genuine examples led to its identification as a forgery. This case underscores the need for advanced scientific methods in authentication.

4. The Becker Forgeries

Background:

- Karl Wilhelm Becker was a notorious German counterfeiter in the early 19th century. He produced forgeries of ancient Greek and Roman coins, which were highly sought after by collectors and museums.

Forgery Case:

- Becker's forgeries were remarkably well-made, often using genuine ancient coin molds. He even marked some of his forgeries with a tiny "KB" to indicate his craftsmanship.

Detection and Outcome:

- Over time, experts identified Becker's forgeries through stylistic analysis, historical research, and the presence of his initials. Many of his forgeries are now collectible in their own right, illustrating the fine line between counterfeit and collectible.

5. The Micro-O Morgan Dollar Forgeries

Background:

- Morgan Dollars are popular among collectors, and rare varieties, such as the 1896-O, 1900-O, and 1902-O, are especially valuable. Counterfeiters have targeted these coins to exploit their high market value.

Forgery Case:

- In the late 20th century, counterfeit Morgan Dollars with a tiny "O" mint mark (smaller than the genuine New Orleans Mint mark) began appearing. These coins were typically produced in China using base metals.

Detection and Outcome:

- The micro-O mint mark was identified using magnification and comparison with genuine coins. Further tests, including weight measurement and metal composition analysis, confirmed these counterfeits. This case highlights the importance of detailed mint mark examination and the challenges posed by international counterfeiting operations.

These case studies illustrate the variety of techniques used by counterfeiters and the methods employed by numismatists to detect fakes. From hidden symbols to advanced scientific analysis, the field of numismatics requires constant vigilance and expertise to protect against forgeries. Understanding these famous cases not only enriches the knowledge of collectors but also prepares them to better identify

and prevent counterfeit coins in their collections.

BOOK 3

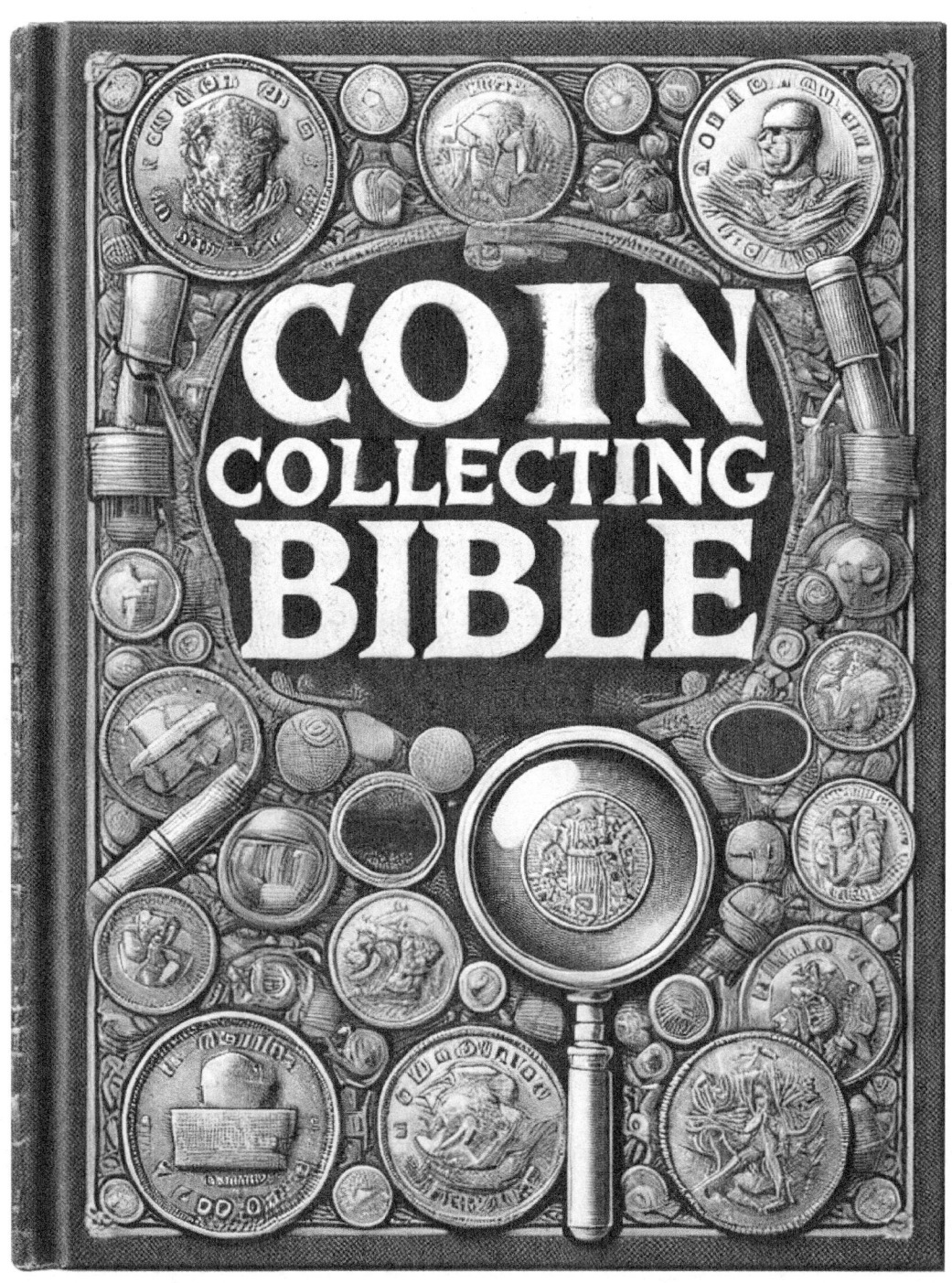

Chapter 1: Minting Process

How Coins Are Minted

The process of minting coins is a fascinating blend of art, history, and technology. From the initial design to the final inspection, each step is crucial to producing high-quality, durable, and aesthetically pleasing coins. Here, we explore the detailed steps involved in the minting process.

1. Designing the Coin

Concept and Artwork:

- **Initial Design:** The process begins with the creation of a design. Artists and engravers work on sketches and concepts, often incorporating themes, historical figures, or national symbols.

- **Approval:** The initial designs are reviewed and approved by various stakeholders, which may include government officials, mint authorities, and sometimes the public.

Digital and Physical Models:

- **Digital Sculpting:** Once the design is approved, it is digitized using computer-aided design (CAD) software. This allows for precise control over the details.

- **Plaster Models:** Traditionally, a large plaster model of the coin design is created. This model is several times larger than the actual coin to allow for intricate detailing.

- **Reduction:** The plaster model is then reduced in size using a machine called a reducing lathe, which transfers the details onto a metal master hub.

2. Creating the Dies

Master Hub and Master Die:

- **Master Hub:** The metal master hub, containing a positive image of the design, is used to create the master die, which holds a negative image of the coin design.

- **Master Die:** The master die is then used to produce working hubs, which are positive images used to create multiple working dies.

Working Dies:

- **Production Dies:** The working hubs strike multiple working dies, which are the tools used to mint the actual coins. Each working die contains a negative image of the coin design.

- **Heat Treatment:** Dies undergo heat treatment to harden them, ensuring they can withstand the pressures of coin striking.

3. Preparing the Planchets

Blanking:

- **Metal Strips:** Coin blanks, also known as planchets, are punched out from large metal strips. These strips are made of specific alloys depending on the coin's denomination and intended use.

- **Quality Control:** The blanks are inspected for any imperfections and weighed to ensure they meet precise standards.

Annealing and Cleaning:

- **Annealing:** The blanks are heated in an annealing furnace to soften the metal, making it easier to strike and reducing the risk of cracking.

- **Cleaning:** After annealing, the blanks are cleaned in a solution to remove any oxides or contaminants, ensuring a smooth surface for striking.

Upsetting:

- **Rim Formation:** The blanks are then run through an upsetting mill, which raises the rim around the edge of the blank. This process helps in forming the coin's design and protects it from wear.

4. Striking the Coins

Coin Presses:

- **High-Pressure Pressing:** The prepared planchets are fed into coin presses, where the working dies strike them with high pressure, transferring the design from the die to the planchet. Modern presses can exert pressures of up to 200 tons and strike hundreds of coins per minute.

- **Single or Multiple Strikes:** Depending on the coin's intended quality, it may be struck once (for regular circulation coins) or multiple times (for proof coins) to ensure sharp details.

Mint Marking:

- **Mint Marks:** During the striking process, mint marks are also applied. These marks indicate the mint where the coin was produced and are often found on a specific part of the coin's design.

5. Inspecting and Packaging

Quality Control:

- **Inspection:** Each batch of coins undergoes rigorous inspection to ensure they meet quality standards. This can involve both automated systems and manual checks by trained inspectors.

- **Defect Removal:** Coins with defects such as improper strikes, blemishes, or incorrect weights are removed from the batch.

Counting and Packaging:

- **Counting:** The coins are then counted using high-speed machines that ensure accuracy.

- **Packaging:** Once counted, the coins are packaged for distribution. Circulating coins are typically bagged in large quantities for transport to banks and other financial institutions, while collector coins might be individually packaged in protective cases.

The minting process is a complex and meticulous procedure that transforms raw metal into finely crafted coins. Each step, from designing and die creation to striking and quality control, ensures that the final product meets strict standards of precision and artistry. Understanding this process not only enhances appreciation for the craftsmanship involved but also highlights the technological advancements that have shaped modern coinage.

Chapter 2: Mint Marks and Their Significance

Mint marks are small letters or symbols on a coin that identify the mint where the coin was produced. These marks hold significant value for collectors and historians, as they provide insights into the coin's origin, rarity, and historical context. Here, we explore the history, purpose, and significance of mint marks in numismatics.

1. History of Mint Marks

Ancient Origins:

- Mint marks date back to ancient times when various cities and regions had their own mints. Greek and Roman coins often featured symbols or letters to denote the mint of origin.

Medieval Period:

- During the medieval period, mint marks became more standardized. European mints used specific symbols, letters, or combinations of both to indicate the place of minting, often to ensure quality and authenticity.

Modern Era:

- In the modern era, particularly in the United States, mint marks became more formalized. The U.S. Mint began using specific letters to denote different mint locations, a practice that continues today.

2. Purpose of Mint Marks

Quality Control:

- Mint marks help in quality control by tracking where coins were minted. This is particularly useful for identifying and addressing issues related to coin production at specific mints.

Authentication:

- Mint marks aid in the authentication of coins. Collectors and numismatists can verify a coin's authenticity and historical accuracy by examining the mint mark.

Rarity and Collectibility:

- Certain mint marks can indicate rarity, making some coins more valuable to collectors. For example, coins from mints that produced fewer coins or were operational for a short period can be highly sought after.

3. Common Mint Marks and Their Locations

United States Mint Marks:

- **Philadelphia (P):** The Philadelphia Mint, established in 1792, is the oldest U.S. Mint. Initially, coins produced here did not bear a mint mark, but later issues, especially those minted for collectors, include a "P."

- **Denver (D):** The Denver Mint, operational since 1906, uses a "D" mint mark.

- **San Francisco (S):** The San Francisco Mint, established in 1854, uses an "S" mint mark. It is known for producing proof coins and special issues.

- **West Point (W):** The West Point Mint, originally a bullion depository, started minting coins in 1984 and uses a "W" mint mark.

Historic U.S. Mint Marks:

- **Carson City (CC):** The Carson City Mint in Nevada, operational from 1870 to 1893, used the "CC" mint mark. Coins from this mint are highly prized by collectors.

- **New Orleans (O):** The New Orleans Mint, operational from 1838 to 1909, used an "O" mint mark.

- **Dahlonega (D) and Charlotte (C):** These Southern mints, operational before the Civil War, used "D" and "C" mint marks, respectively. They mainly produced gold coins.

4. Significance of Mint Marks in Numismatics

Collectibility:

- Coins with specific mint marks can be more collectible and valuable. For example, the 1909-S VDB Lincoln Cent from the San Francisco Mint is a famous key date coin, highly sought after by collectors due to its low mintage and distinctive mint mark.

Historical Context:

- Mint marks provide historical context. Coins from certain mints during specific periods can tell stories about economic conditions, regional developments, and historical events. For instance, coins minted at the Carson City Mint reflect the Nevada silver rush era.

Identification and Attribution:

- Mint marks help in the accurate identification and attribution of coins. This is essential for cataloging, pricing, and understanding the provenance of a coin.

Error Coins:

- Error coins involving mint marks, such as over-mint marks (where one mint mark is struck over another), are particularly interesting to collectors and can significantly increase a coin's value.

5. Notable Examples of Mint Mark Usage

1943 Copper Cents:

- During World War II, most U.S. pennies were struck in steel to save copper for the war effort. However, a few 1943 cents were mistakenly struck in copper. The mint marks (or lack thereof) on these rare coins help identify their origins and validate their authenticity.

Morgan Silver Dollars:

- Morgan Silver Dollars were minted in several locations, including Philadelphia, Denver, San Francisco, Carson City, and New Orleans. The mint marks on these coins are crucial for determining their rarity and value. For example, the 1889-CC Morgan Dollar is one of the rarest and most valuable coins in the series.

Modern Commemoratives:

- Modern commemorative coins often feature mint marks to denote special issues from specific mints, adding to their collectibility and historical interest.

Mint marks are small but significant details that play a crucial role in the world of coin collecting and numismatics. They provide essential information about a coin's origin, authenticity, and historical context, making them a vital aspect of coin evaluation and appreciation. Collectors and historians alike rely on mint marks to uncover the rich stories behind each coin, enhancing both their monetary and historical value.

Chapter 3: Error Coins and Varieties in Numismatics

Error coins and varieties are fascinating anomalies in the minting process that result in coins differing from the intended design or production standards. These deviations can range from minor imperfections to major errors, and they often increase the collectibility and value of the affected coins. Here, we explore the types of error coins and varieties commonly found in numismatics.

1. Types of Error Coins

a. Planchet Errors:

- **Blank Planchet Errors:** These errors occur when planchets (coin blanks) are improperly prepared or are of incorrect composition.

  - ○ **Wrong Planchet:** A coin struck on a planchet intended for another denomination or metal type.

  - ○ **Clipped Planchet:** Portions of the planchet are missing due to improper punching or blanking.

- **Off-Metal Errors:** Coins struck on planchets made from a different metal than intended.

  - ○ **Wrong Metal:** For example, a copper coin struck on a planchet intended for a silver coin.

b. Die Errors:

- **Die Variety Errors:** Errors resulting from issues with the dies used to strike the coins.

  - o **Die Crack:** A small crack develops on the die, causing a raised line on the struck coin.

  - o **Die Clash:** Impressions of the design intended for one side of the coin are transferred to the other side due to misalignment or accidental contact of dies.

- **Doubled Dies:** This occurs when the hubbing process causes the design to be doubled, resulting in a doubled appearance on the coin's features.

  - o **Class I Doubled Die:** Shows strong doubling on the entire design.

  - o **Class II Doubled Die:** Shows doubling primarily on the lettering and digits.

  - o **Class III Doubled Die:** Shows doubling on the design in a rotated manner.

c. Striking Errors:

- **Off-Center Strikes:** Coins that are struck off-center, resulting in part of the design missing or partially struck.

- **Broadstrike:** Occurs when the coin fails to be properly restrained by the collar and expands beyond its intended diameter.

- **Brockage:** A type of error where a coin sticks to the die after striking and becomes impressed on another planchet, creating a mirror image.

d. Miscellaneous Errors:

- **Struck Through Errors:** Occurs when foreign objects such as cloth, grease, or debris are struck into the coin.

- **Cud Errors:** A chunk of the coin's surface breaks off from the edge due to a damaged die.

2. Varieties in Coinage

a. Minor Varieties:

- **Variations in Design Elements:** Minor differences in design elements such as lettering size, placement, or style.

- **Date Varieties:** Changes in the positioning or style of date digits on the coin.

b. Major Varieties:

- **Overdates:** Coins where a digit or letter from a previous year's die was not completely removed before punching a new date.

- **Re-punched Mint Marks:** Mint marks that were punched more than once on the die, resulting in visible traces or shadows of previous placements.

c. Transitional Errors:

- **Coins of Two Years:** Coins struck using dies of different years accidentally mixed.

- **Wrong Design:** Coins with an earlier or later design used unintentionally.

3. Collectibility and Value

Error coins and varieties are highly collectible among numismatists due to their rarity, uniqueness, and historical interest. The value of these coins is influenced by factors such as the severity of the error, the coin's overall condition, demand from collectors, and the historical significance of the error.

Examples of Famous Error Coins:

- **1955 Doubled Die Lincoln Cent:** Known for its strong doubling in the lettering and date.

- **1943 Copper Lincoln Cent:** Struck on copper planchets left over from 1942, a few escaped the mint and are highly sought after.

- **1982 No Mint Mark Roosevelt Dime:** Produced when a Denver Mint die was used without the mint mark, creating a rare variety.

4. Detecting and Authenticating Error Coins

Detecting error coins requires careful examination and knowledge of minting processes and coin characteristics. Methods include visual inspection under magnification, comparison with known genuine examples, checking for diagnostic features of specific errors, and sometimes using specialized equipment for metal composition analysis.

Authentication: Professional coin grading services and experienced numismatists can provide authentication and grading services for error coins, certifying their authenticity and providing an estimate of their market value.

Error coins and varieties add an exciting dimension to coin collecting, offering collectors the opportunity to acquire unique and historically significant pieces. Understanding the types of errors and varieties, their causes, and their collectibility enhances appreciation for the art and science of coin production. Whether minor deviations or major anomalies, error coins continue to captivate collectors worldwide, showcasing the fascinating world of numismatic anomalies and the stories they tell about coin production throughout history.

BOOK 4

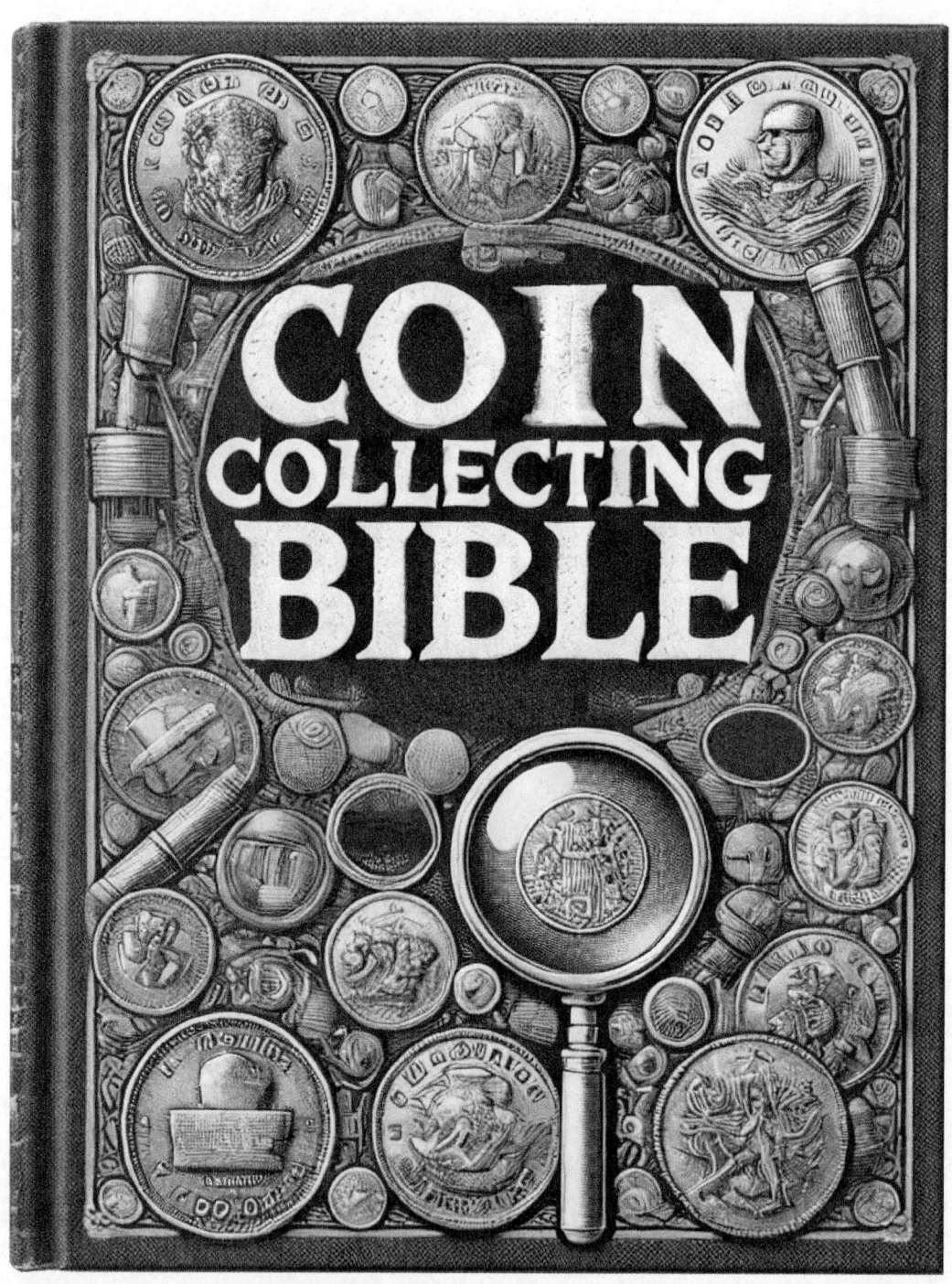

Chapter 1: Coin Design and Artistry

Evolution of Coin Designs

The evolution of coin designs reflects not only artistic trends but also cultural, technological, and historical influences throughout different eras and civilizations. From ancient times to modern coinage, the design of coins has evolved significantly, each period leaving its mark on the numismatic landscape. Here, we explore the fascinating journey of coin design, highlighting key developments and influences over time.

1. Ancient and Classical Period

Greek and Roman Coinage:

- **Artistic Depictions:** Ancient Greek coins often featured gods, goddesses, mythological figures, and symbols of city-states. They were meticulously crafted, showcasing high relief and intricate designs that symbolized cultural and political identity.

- **Portraiture:** Roman coins introduced portraiture of rulers and emperors, reflecting their authority and status. These portraits evolved over time, showing changes in fashion, age, and propaganda purposes.

Byzantine Coinage:

- **Christian Symbolism:** Byzantine coins adopted Christian symbols such as the cross, Chi-Rho, and religious figures. They were characterized by elaborate designs and inscriptions in Greek.

2. Medieval and Renaissance Period

Medieval European Coinage:

- **Heraldic Designs:** Medieval coins often featured heraldic symbols of ruling families, coats of arms, and regional emblems. These designs served as political statements and identifiers of authority.

Renaissance and Baroque Influence:

- **Classical Revival:** During the Renaissance, coin designs were influenced by classical art and architecture. Coins depicted allegorical figures, idealized portraits, and intricate border patterns, showcasing a renewed interest in classical aesthetics.

3. Early Modern Era

Colonial and Early American Coinage:

- **Simplicity and Utility:** Early American coins were primarily utilitarian, featuring simple designs such as colonial symbols, state seals, and numerical denominations. They lacked the elaborate artistry seen in European counterparts.

European Expansion:

- **Global Influences:** As European powers expanded globally, coin designs incorporated cultural motifs and symbols from colonies and trade routes. This period marked the fusion of diverse artistic styles and influences.

4. Modern Era

Industrial Revolution and Technological Advancements:

- **Mechanization:** The Industrial Revolution introduced mechanized minting processes, allowing for more standardized designs and mass production. Coins featured national symbols, political leaders, and industrial motifs.

Art Deco and Modernism:

- **Geometric Designs:** In the early 20th century, coin designs embraced Art Deco and modernist principles, characterized by geometric shapes, simplified forms, and abstract motifs. This era emphasized functionality and aesthetic appeal.

5. Contemporary Coinage

Cultural Diversity and Innovation:

- **Diverse Themes:** Modern coins reflect global cultural diversity, featuring themes such as wildlife, landmarks, historical events, and advancements in science and technology.

- **Commemorative Issues:** Specialized coins commemorate significant anniversaries, events, and achievements, showcasing innovative designs and techniques such as colorization and holography.

6. Technological Advances in Coin Design

Digital Design Tools:

- **Computer-Aided Design (CAD):** Modern coin designers utilize CAD software for precise detailing, allowing for intricate patterns, textures, and three-dimensional simulations before production.

Anti-Counterfeiting Measures:

- **Security Features:** Advanced minting technologies incorporate security features such as micro-engraving, holograms, and laser marking to deter counterfeiting and enhance coin authentication.

7. Global Influence and Collaboration

International Design Competitions:

- **Cross-Cultural Exchange:** Countries participate in international design competitions to create innovative and culturally significant coin designs. Winning designs often reflect collaborative efforts and artistic excellence.

8. Collectibility and Cultural Significance

Collector Appeal:

- **Artistic Value:** Collectors value coins not only for their historical and monetary significance but also for their artistic merit and aesthetic appeal.

- **Educational Value:** Coin designs provide insights into a nation's history, culture, and values, serving as tangible artifacts of societal evolution.

The evolution of coin designs spans millennia and continents, reflecting the artistic, cultural, and technological advancements of each era. From ancient symbols and allegorical figures to modern innovations in design and security, coins continue to be both functional currency and miniature works of art. The study of coin design not only enriches numismatic knowledge but also offers a glimpse into the broader tapestry of human creativity and historical narrative. As numismatics evolves, so too will the diversity and complexity of coin designs, ensuring their enduring appeal to collectors and enthusiasts worldwide.

Chapter 2: Notable Coin Designers and Engravers

Throughout history, numerous artists, engravers, and designers have made significant contributions to the world of numismatics through their creativity, skill, and innovative designs. Their work has shaped the aesthetics and cultural significance of coins, making them highly collectible and admired. Here are some notable coin designers and engravers renowned for their contributions:

1. Augustus Saint-Gaudens (1848-1907)

Notable Works:

- **Saint-Gaudens Double Eagle (1907-1933):** Perhaps his most famous design, featuring Liberty striding forward with rays of sun and a torch in her hand, symbolizing freedom and progress.

- **Indian Head Eagle (1907-1933):** The $10 gold coin designed with a Native American chief in profile, considered a masterpiece of American coinage.

Impact:

- Saint-Gaudens revolutionized American coin design during the early 20th century, emphasizing artistic integrity and classical aesthetics. His designs remain iconic and highly coveted among collectors.

2. John Mercanti (1943-present)

Notable Works:

- **American Silver Eagle Reverse (1986-2021):** Mercanti designed the reverse side of the American Silver Eagle bullion coin, featuring a heraldic eagle with shield, arrows, and olive branch.

- **Other U.S. Coins:** Mercanti has designed numerous commemorative coins and medal series for the United States Mint, showcasing his skill in detailed engraving and design.

Impact:

- As the 12th Chief Engraver of the U.S. Mint, Mercanti's designs are highly influential in contemporary American numismatics, known for their precision and artistic flair.

3. Thomas Pesendorfer (1952-present)

Notable Works:

- **Austrian Euro Coins:** Pesendorfer is known for his designs on Austrian euro coins, including national sides featuring cultural landmarks, historical figures, and natural landscapes.

- **Gold and Silver Commemorative Coins:** He has also designed numerous gold and silver commemorative coins for Austria, combining traditional and modern artistic elements.

Impact:

- Pesendorfer's designs reflect a blend of cultural heritage and contemporary aesthetics, contributing to the visual identity of Austrian coinage in the European context.

4. Emanuel Hahn (1881-1957)

Notable Works:

- **Canadian Coins:** Hahn designed several iconic Canadian coins, including the Bluenose schooner on the Canadian dime and the caribou on the Canadian quarter.

- **Commemorative Medals:** His work extended to commemorative medals, sculptures, and architectural pieces, showcasing his versatility as an artist.

Impact:

- Hahn's designs are deeply ingrained in Canadian numismatic history, representing national pride and cultural identity through his depictions of Canadian wildlife and maritime heritage.

5. Luc Luycx (1958-present)

Notable Works:

- **Euro Coins:** Luycx is the designer of the common reverse side of the euro coins, featuring a map of Europe with the denomination placed on top of it.

- **Belgian Coin Designs:** He has also designed several coins for Belgium, incorporating national symbols, historical figures, and landmarks.

Impact:

- Luycx's design for the euro coins is one of the most widely recognized in modern European numismatics, symbolizing the unity and diversity of the European Union.

6. Laura Gardin Fraser (1889-1966)

Notable Works:

- **Oregon Trail Memorial Half Dollar (1926):** Fraser designed this commemorative coin featuring a Native American and a pioneer facing left, symbolizing westward expansion.

- **Suffragist Commemorative Half Dollar (1920):** She also designed the first U.S. coin to feature a real woman—Liberty—with a tiara of stars.

Impact:

- Fraser was a pioneer herself in American coin design, known for her detailed and historically significant designs that celebrated American themes and achievements.

7. Robert Scot (1745-1823)

Notable Works:

- **Early American Coinage:** Scot was the first Chief Engraver of the United States Mint and designed the Draped Bust series of coins, including the silver dollar and half dollar.

- **Flowing Hair Dollar (1794-1795):** He engraved the first official U.S. silver dollar, featuring a portrait of Liberty with flowing hair.

Impact:

- Scot's designs established the visual identity of early American coinage, setting a precedent for subsequent generations of American coin designers.

These notable coin designers and engravers have left an indelible mark on numismatics through their creativity, technical skill, and dedication to artistic excellence. Their designs not only adorn coins but also tell stories of culture, history, and national identity. Collectors and enthusiasts continue to cherish their work, making their coins highly sought after in the world of numismatics. As the field of coin design evolves, these artists' legacies continue to inspire new generations of designers to push the boundaries of artistic expression in coinage.

Chapter 3: Symbolism and Motifs on Coins

Coins serve not only as a means of commerce but also as miniature works of art that convey cultural, political, and historical messages through symbolism and motifs. Throughout history, various symbols and motifs have been used on coins to represent a nation's identity, values, and aspirations. Here, we explore the significance and common themes of symbolism and motifs found on coins.

1. National Identity and Sovereignty

National Emblems:

- **Coats of Arms:** Many coins feature national coats of arms, representing sovereignty and authority. These heraldic designs often include shields, crests, and mottoes that symbolize the country's unity and heritage.

- **Flags:** Flags and national banners are depicted on coins to symbolize patriotism and national pride, highlighting important historical events or national achievements.

2. Historical Figures and Monarchs

Portraits:

- **Rulers and Leaders:** Coins often bear portraits of monarchs, presidents, or historical figures who played significant roles in shaping a nation's history. These portraits serve as symbols of authority and leadership.

- **Monetary Reform:** Changes in coin designs often coincide with shifts in political power or monetary reforms, reflecting transitions in governance and national identity.

3. Allegorical and Mythological Figures

Personifications:

- **Allegorical Representations:** Allegorical figures such as Liberty, Justice, and Victory are commonly depicted on coins to embody abstract concepts and national ideals. These personifications evoke themes of freedom, justice, and triumph.

- **Mythological Symbols:** Ancient coins often feature gods, goddesses, and mythical creatures from classical mythology, symbolizing religious beliefs, cultural values, and divine protection.

4. Cultural Heritage and Traditions

Cultural Symbols:

- **Architecture and Landmarks:** Coins showcase iconic buildings, monuments, and landmarks that symbolize cultural heritage and national identity. These symbols promote tourism and celebrate architectural achievements.

- **Ethnic Diversity:** Coins may depict cultural diversity through symbols of indigenous tribes, ethnic groups, or traditional attire, celebrating multiculturalism and unity within a nation.

5. Natural Resources and Wildlife

Flora and Fauna:

- **Native Plants:** Coins often feature native flora such as flowers, trees, and crops that symbolize agricultural abundance and environmental stewardship.

- **Wildlife:** Animals and birds native to the region are depicted on coins to highlight biodiversity, conservation efforts, and ecological significance.

6. Commemorative Themes and Events

Historical Events:

- **Anniversaries and Milestones:** Commemorative coins mark significant anniversaries, historical events, and milestones in a nation's history. These coins serve as reminders of cultural achievements and collective memory.

- **War and Peace:** Coins may commemorate military victories, peace treaties, or wartime sacrifices, honoring the courage and resilience of individuals and nations.

7. Economic and Technological Progress

Symbols of Prosperity:

- **Industry and Innovation:** Coins depict symbols of economic prosperity, such as factories, machinery, and technological advancements. These motifs signify industrial growth and technological innovation.

- **Trade and Commerce:** Symbols of trade routes, ships, and global connections on coins reflect international trade relationships and economic interdependence.

8. Unity and Diversity

Unity in Diversity:

- **Unity Symbols:** Coins may feature symbols of unity, such as clasped hands, intertwined circles, or chains, representing solidarity and cooperation among diverse communities.

- **Multinational Coins:** International coins, such as those issued by the European Union, feature motifs that symbolize unity, collaboration, and shared values among member states.

Symbolism and motifs on coins encapsulate the rich tapestry of human history, culture, and aspirations. They serve as powerful tools for storytelling, conveying complex ideas and values in a visual and accessible form. Whether portraying national sovereignty, celebrating cultural heritage, or commemorating pivotal events, these symbols on coins transcend their monetary value to inspire reflection, pride, and appreciation for the diverse narratives that shape our world. Numismatists and collectors cherish coins not only for their historical and artistic merit but also for their role in preserving and interpreting the shared heritage of humanity.

BOOK 5

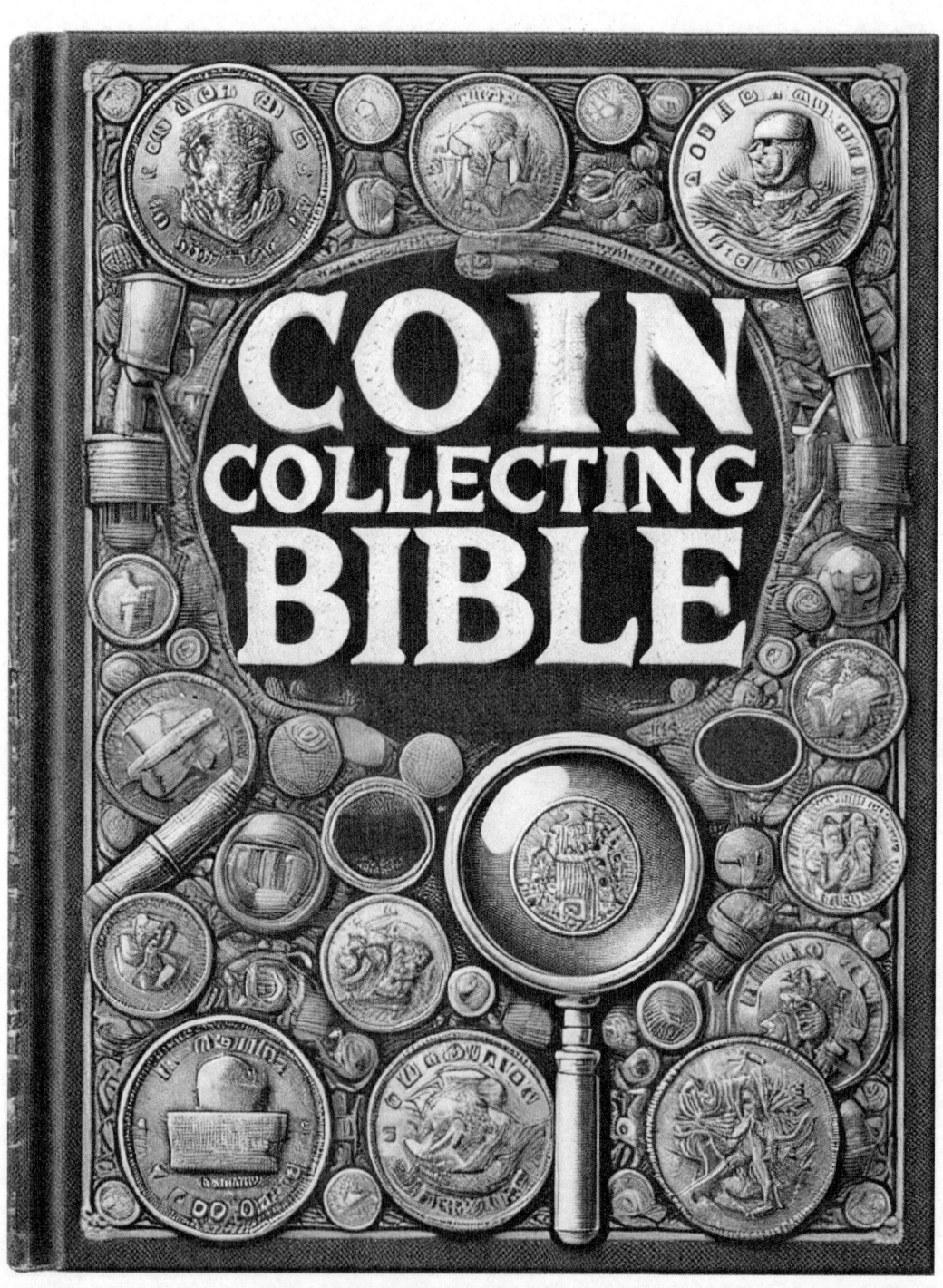

Chapter 1: Coin Grading

Grading Systems and Methods

Coin grading is a crucial aspect of numismatics that evaluates the condition and quality of coins, determining their market value, rarity, and desirability among collectors. Various grading systems have been developed over time to standardize the assessment process and provide consistency in coin grading. Here, we delve into the grading systems, focusing on the renowned Sheldon scale and other methodologies used in numismatics.

1. The Sheldon Scale

Introduction:

- The Sheldon Scale, named after its creator Dr. William Herbert Sheldon, is one of the most widely used grading systems for coins. It assigns a numerical grade from 1 to 70 to assess a coin's condition, with 70 being a perfect or pristine specimen.

Key Grades:

- **Poor (PO-1 to PO-3):** Barely identifiable features due to heavy wear and damage.

- **Fair (FR-2 to FR-4):** Details are visible but very worn with flatness evident on major devices.

- **Good (G-4 to G-6):** Design details are outlined but heavily worn.

- **Very Good (VG-8 to VG-10):** Moderate wear with full rims and clear but flattened details.

- **Fine (F-12 to F-15):** Moderate wear with complete lettering and major features visible.

- **Very Fine (VF-20 to VF-35):** Minor wear with some finer details remaining and full legends readable.

- **Extremely Fine (EF or XF-40 to XF-45):** Light wear with slight traces of mint luster and sharp details.

- **About Uncirculated (AU-50 to AU-58):** Light wear with traces of luster in protected areas.

- **Uncirculated (MS or Mint State):**

   - **MS-60 to MS-70:** No wear with varying degrees of mint brilliance and sharp details, with MS-70 being perfect.

Application:

- Numismatists and professional graders use magnification, lighting, and experience to determine the grade based on wear, strikes, luster, surface preservation, and eye appeal.

2. Other Grading Systems

NGC (Numismatic Guaranty Corporation) and PCGS (Professional Coin Grading Service):

- These are two of the most prominent third-party grading services that use a numerical scale similar to the Sheldon Scale but also include additional descriptors for surface quality and eye appeal.

- **Designations:** Both services use designations like Proof (PR or PF) for coins struck with specially polished dies and blanks, or Cameo (CAM or DCAM) for coins with frosted devices against mirror-like fields.

European Grading Systems:

- **UK Grading:** Grades range from Poor (P) to Brilliant Uncirculated (BU) with varying descriptors for quality and condition.

- **German Grading:** Uses a scale from Sehr Schön (SS) for very good to Stempelglanz (ST) for brilliant uncirculated.

Japanese Grading System:

- **Shu-Ka-Ichi (S-K-I):** This system categorizes coins from Shu (uncirculated) to Ka (almost uncirculated) to Ichi (fine).

3. Factors Affecting Grading

Wear and Tear:

- **High Points:** Wear is often most noticeable on high points of the coin's design.

- **Fields and Devices:** Examination of fields (flat surfaces) and devices (raised portions) helps determine wear patterns and overall preservation.

Surface Preservation:

- **Marks and Blemishes:** Graders assess the presence of scratches, nicks, stains, or other imperfections that affect the coin's surface quality.

- **Cleaning and Alterations:** Signs of cleaning, polishing, or artificial toning can detract from a coin's grade and value.

4. Importance of Grading

Market Value:

- Grading significantly influences a coin's market value, with higher grades commanding premium prices due to rarity and condition.

Authentication:

- Professional grading services authenticate coins, providing certification of authenticity and protection against counterfeiting.

Collector Confidence:

- Consistent grading instills confidence among collectors and investors, ensuring fair transactions and accurate representation of a coin's condition.

Coin grading systems, such as the Sheldon Scale and its derivatives, play a crucial role in determining the quality, value, and marketability of coins in the numismatic world. By providing standardized assessments based on wear, preservation, and eye appeal, these systems enable collectors, investors, and dealers to make informed decisions and accurately appraise the worth of coins. As numismatic techniques and technologies evolve, grading systems continue to adapt, maintaining their relevance in preserving the integrity and historical significance of coins for future generations.

Chapter 2: Factors Affecting Coin Grade: Wear, Luster, Preservation

Coin grading is a specialized skill that involves assessing a coin's condition based on several key factors. These factors collectively determine the coin's grade, which in turn influences its market value and desirability among collectors. Understanding how wear, luster, and preservation impact coin grading provides insight into the nuanced evaluation process conducted by numismatists and professional graders.

1. Wear

Definition and Types of Wear:

- **Wear** refers to the loss of metal from a coin's surface due to circulation, handling, or environmental factors over time. It is a crucial aspect of grading as it directly affects the visibility and definition of a coin's design elements.

- **Types of Wear:** Coins exhibit wear differently based on their circulation history:

  o **High-Point Wear:** Most noticeable on the raised portions of the coin's design, such as the portrait, lettering, or detailed features.

o **Even Wear:** Uniform wear across the coin's surface, indicating prolonged circulation without significant damage.

o **Rim Wear:** Wear along the edges of the coin due to contact with other coins or surfaces.

Impact on Grade:

- **Higher Grades:** Coins in higher grades (e.g., Mint State or Uncirculated grades) typically show minimal to no wear. They retain sharp details with full mint luster, indicating a well-preserved specimen.

- **Lower Grades:** Coins with substantial wear receive lower grades (e.g., About Good to Very Fine grades). Design elements may be flattened, and details are less distinct due to wear.

2. Luster

Definition and Types of Luster:

- **Luster** refers to the shine or reflective quality of a coin's surface, caused by the way light interacts with the metal. It is a critical indicator of a coin's originality and overall appeal.

- **Types of Lusters:**

o **Cartwheel Luster:** Describes the radiant effect observed on coins when tilted under light, resembling the spokes of a cartwheel. It is characteristic of coins with a high metallic sheen.

    ○ **Proof Luster:** Found on proof coins, this type of luster is exceptionally smooth and mirror-like, reflecting superior craftsmanship and preparation of dies and planchets.

Impact on Grade:

- **High-Grade Coins:** Coins with full, unbroken luster (e.g., MS-65 to MS-70) are highly coveted by collectors and command premium prices. They exhibit a vibrant appearance and pristine surfaces.

- **Diminished Luster:** Coins with reduced or impaired luster (e.g., AU-50 to XF-45) may receive lower grades, as the loss of luster detracts from their visual appeal and perceived originality.

3. Preservation

Definition and Factors Considered:

- **Preservation** refers to the overall physical condition and appearance of a coin, encompassing factors such as surface quality, cleanliness, and absence of damage or flaws.

- **Factors Considered:**

    ○ **Surface Marks:** Includes scratches, abrasions, spots, or discolorations that affect the coin's appearance and grade.

    ○ **Environmental Damage:** Toning, corrosion, or oxidation caused by exposure to moisture, chemicals, or improper storage can impact a coin's preservation.

○ **Cleaning and Alterations:** Signs of cleaning, polishing, or artificial toning can diminish a coin's grade and authenticity.

Impact on Grade:

- **Well-Preserved Coins:** Coins with excellent preservation (e.g., MS-60 to MS-70) exhibit minimal surface distractions and retain their original appearance. They are highly sought after by collectors for their superior condition.

- **Impaired Preservation:** Coins with significant issues (e.g., AG-3 to VG-8) may receive lower grades due to impaired surface quality, which detracts from their overall appeal and collector value.

4. Additional Considerations

Strike Quality:

- The quality of a coin's strike refers to the sharpness and definition of its design elements, including details and edges. A well-struck coin enhances its visual appeal and grade.

Eye Appeal:

- Subjective factors such as overall attractiveness, toning patterns, and aesthetic appeal also influence a coin's grade. Coins with exceptional eye appeal may receive higher grades despite minor imperfections.

5. Coin Grading Process

Methodology:

- **Examination:** Numismatists and professional graders use specialized tools such as magnification, lighting, and grading standards to assess each coin's condition thoroughly.

- **Criteria:** Graders evaluate multiple aspects, including wear patterns, surface marks, luster quality, strike characteristics, and overall preservation.

- **Comparison:** Coins are compared against established grading scales (e.g., Sheldon Scale, numeric scales used by grading services like NGC and PCGS) to assign a grade that accurately reflects its condition.

Certification Services:

- **Third-Party Grading:** Many coins are submitted to third-party grading services like NGC (Numismatic Guaranty Corporation) or PCGS (Professional Coin Grading Service) for independent, unbiased assessment and certification.

- **Authentication:** These services also provide authentication of a coin's genuineness, adding to its market credibility and ensuring transparency in transactions.

6. Importance of Coin Grading

Market Value:

- **Determining Value:** The assigned grade significantly impacts a coin's market value and pricing. Higher grades command higher premiums due to rarity, condition, and collector demand.

- **Market Confidence:** Consistent grading practices instill confidence among collectors, investors, and dealers, facilitating fair and informed buying, selling, and trading of coins.

Historical and Cultural Preservation:

- **Preserving History:** Grading helps preserve the historical and cultural significance of coins by documenting their condition at specific points in time.

- **Educational Value:** Graded coins serve as educational tools, illustrating the evolution of minting techniques, design aesthetics, and historical events.

7. Evolution of Coin Grading

Technological Advances:

- **Digital Imaging:** High-resolution digital imaging and photography enhance the ability to capture and document minute details of coins for grading purposes.

- **Grading Software:** Advanced grading software assists in standardizing assessments and minimizing human error in grading.

Global Standardization:

- **International Recognition:** Grading scales and practices are increasingly standardized globally, facilitating cross-border transactions and promoting consistency in grading standards.

Grading coins involves a detailed assessment of wear, luster, preservation, and other factors to determine their condition and grade accurately. Numismatists rely on standardized grading scales and professional expertise to provide consistent evaluations that guide collectors, investors, and dealers in assessing the value and authenticity of coins. Understanding these factors not only enhances appreciation for the artistry and history encapsulated in coins but also ensures fair transactions and preservation of numismatic integrity across the global collecting community. As coin grading methodologies continue to evolve with advancements in technology and grading standards, these fundamental factors remain essential in evaluating and interpreting the beauty and significance of coins throughout history.

BOOK 6

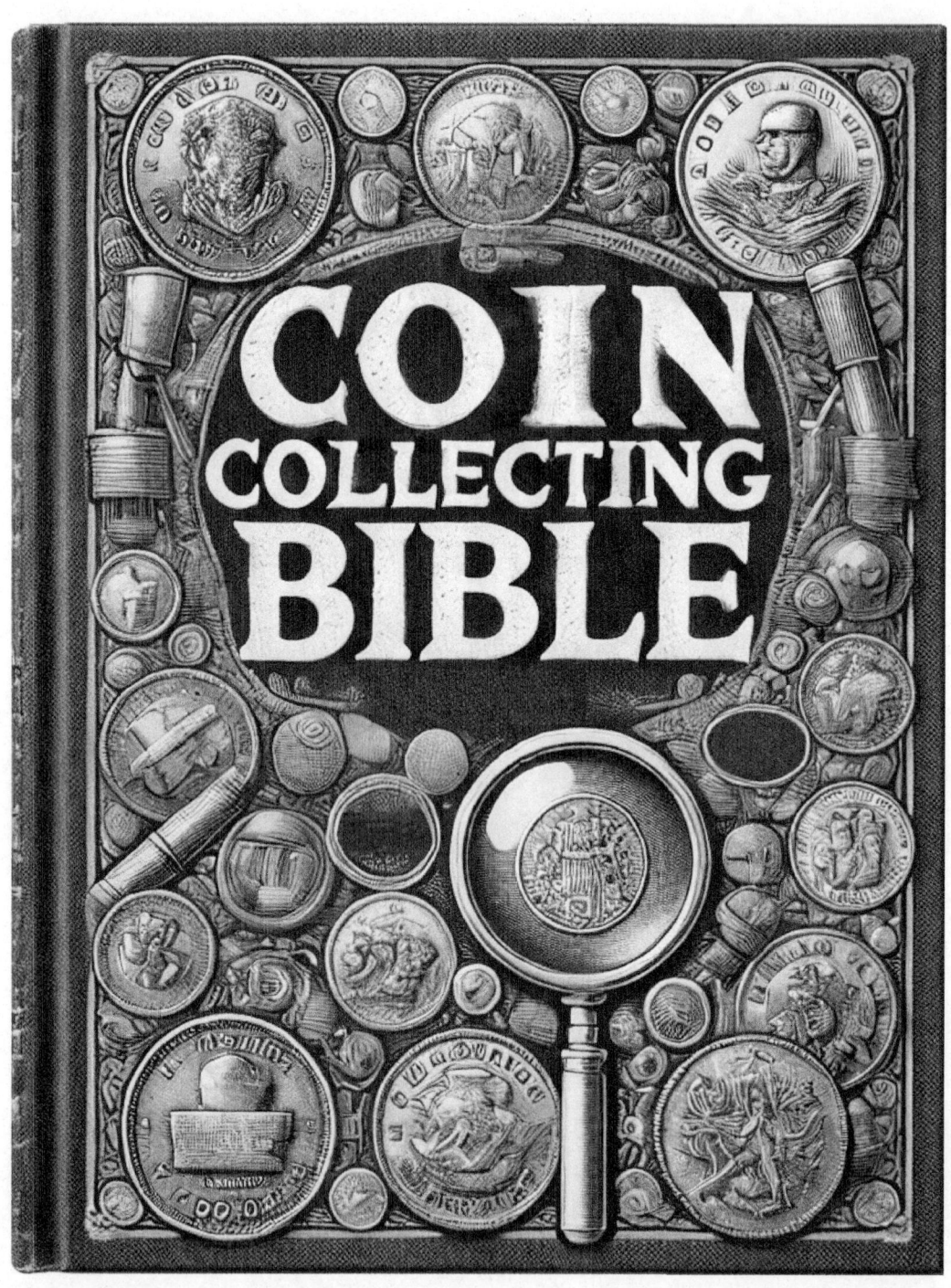

Chapter 1: Coin Valuation

Determining Coin Values

Determining the value of coins is a nuanced process that integrates various factors to establish their market worth accurately. Numismatists and collectors rely on a combination of methodologies, including price guides, auction results, professional appraisals, and market trends, to evaluate coins effectively. Here's a detailed exploration of these aspects:

1. Price Guides

Definition and Types:

- **Price guides** are comprehensive references that provide estimated values for coins based on their condition, rarity, and demand among collectors.

- **Printed Guides:** Publications like the Red Book (A Guidebook of United States Coins) or the Standard Catalog of World Coins offer detailed listings and valuations for various coin series and types.

- **Online Resources:** Websites and databases such as NumisMedia, NGC Price Guide, and PCGS Price Guide provide real-time updates and historical data, allowing collectors to access current market values and trends.

Factors Considered in Price Guides:

- **Grade:** The condition of a coin significantly influences its value. Coins in higher grades (e.g., Mint State or Proof) typically command higher prices due to their superior preservation and appeal.

- **Rarity:** Coins with low mintage figures or those featuring unique attributes are often more valuable. Rarity enhances a coin's desirability among collectors and investors.

- **Market Demand:** Current trends and collector interest play a crucial role in determining a coin's value. Popular series or coins with historical significance may see increased demand and higher prices.

2. Auction Results

Role in Valuation:

- **Auctions** provide real-time market insights into coin values by showcasing actual sale prices achieved for coins.

- **Leading Auction Houses:** Institutions like Heritage Auctions, Stack's Bowers Galleries, and Sotheby's conduct numismatic auctions worldwide, setting benchmarks for coin values.

- **Factors Impacting Auction Results:**

  - **Quality and Condition:** Coins in exceptional condition or with unique features often attract competitive bidding and achieve premium prices.

- o **Historical Significance:** Coins linked to notable events, famous collections, or cultural milestones may command higher values due to their historical context and provenance.

- o **Buyer Dynamics:** Auction dynamics, including the number of interested bidders and their willingness to pay, influence final sale prices.

3. Professional Appraisal

Role of Appraisers:

- **Numismatic Experts:** Professional appraisers offer specialized evaluations based on their expertise in grading, market knowledge, and historical context.

- **Authentication and Verification:** Appraisers verify the authenticity of coins and assess their condition thoroughly, providing detailed reports for insurance, estate planning, or investment purposes.

- **Methods Used:**

  - o **Grading Standards:** Utilizing established grading scales such as the Sheldon Scale, NGC, or PCGS standards to assess a coin's condition objectively.

  - o **Market Insight:** Drawing on extensive market data, recent auction results, and collector preferences to provide accurate valuations reflective of current market conditions.

Chapter 2: Market Trends and Conditions

Volatility and Stability:

- **Market Dynamics:** Coin values can fluctuate due to economic factors, changes in collector preferences, or shifts in global numismatic trends.

- **Investment Potential:** Some coins may serve as investments, with potential for value appreciation over time based on rarity, historical significance, and broader market conditions.

6. Professional Appraisal

Role of Appraisers:

- **Numismatic Experts:** Professional appraisers play a critical role in assessing the value of coins accurately. They bring specialized knowledge of numismatics, including grading standards, market trends, and historical context.

- **Authentication and Verification:** Appraisers verify the authenticity of coins through detailed examination, ensuring they are genuine and not counterfeit or altered.

- **Methods Used:**

  - **Grading Expertise:** Utilizing standardized grading scales such as the Sheldon Scale (for US coins) or international standards like those used by NGC and PCGS to determine the condition of coins objectively.

○ **Market Insight:** Drawing on extensive data from auction results, historical sales, and collector preferences to provide a comprehensive valuation reflective of current market conditions.

Appraisal Reports:

- **Documentation:** Appraisers provide detailed reports outlining their assessment process, findings, and the rationale behind the assigned value.

- **Purpose:** These reports are crucial for insurance purposes, estate planning, or when buying or selling high-value coins to ensure transparency and accuracy in transactions.

7. Market Trends and Conditions

Factors Influencing Coin Values:

- **Economic Factors:** Economic stability, inflation rates, and overall market conditions can impact the value of coins as alternative investments.

- **Collector Trends:** Shifts in collector interests, such as emerging trends in specific coin series or historical periods, influence demand and prices.

- **Global Events:** Significant events or anniversaries related to coins or historical figures can spark renewed interest and affect market values.

Volatility and Stability:

- **Market Fluctuations:** Coin values may experience fluctuations over time due to changes in supply and demand dynamics, investor sentiment, or external economic factors.

- **Stability in Rarity:** Rare coins with stable provenance and documented histories tend to maintain or increase their value steadily over the long term.

8. Rarity and Condition

Critical Assessment Criteria:

- **Rarity:** The scarcity of a coin relative to its total mintage or surviving population is a primary determinant of its value. Coins with low mintages, key dates, or limited surviving specimens often command higher prices.

- **Condition:** The state of preservation significantly impacts a coin's appeal and value. Coins in pristine condition with minimal wear, attractive toning, and full mint luster are highly sought after by collectors.

9. Investment Considerations

Long-Term Potential:

- **Collectible Value:** Many coins are acquired not only for their aesthetic and historical appeal but also as potential long-term investments. Coins with strong collector bases and historical significance may appreciate in value over time.

- **Diversification:** Including rare coins in an investment portfolio can provide diversification benefits, potentially offering protection against economic downturns and currency fluctuations.

Professional Advice:

- **Consultation:** Investors and collectors often seek guidance from numismatic experts or financial advisors specializing in alternative investments to make informed decisions regarding coin acquisitions and sales.

- **Due Diligence:** Conducting thorough research, staying informed about market trends, and seeking professional appraisals are essential steps in ensuring sound investment decisions in numismatics.

Evaluating coin values requires a multifaceted approach that integrates expertise in numismatics, comprehensive market analysis, and an understanding of collector preferences and historical contexts. By utilizing price guides, auction results, professional appraisals, and staying informed about market trends, collectors and investors can navigate the dynamic landscape of numismatic investments effectively. Understanding the factors influencing coin values enables individuals to make informed decisions, preserve the integrity of their collections, and potentially capitalize on investment opportunities in the evolving world of numismatics. As the market continues to evolve, maintaining a proactive and informed approach remains key to maximizing the value and enjoyment derived from coin collecting and investment.

BOOK 7

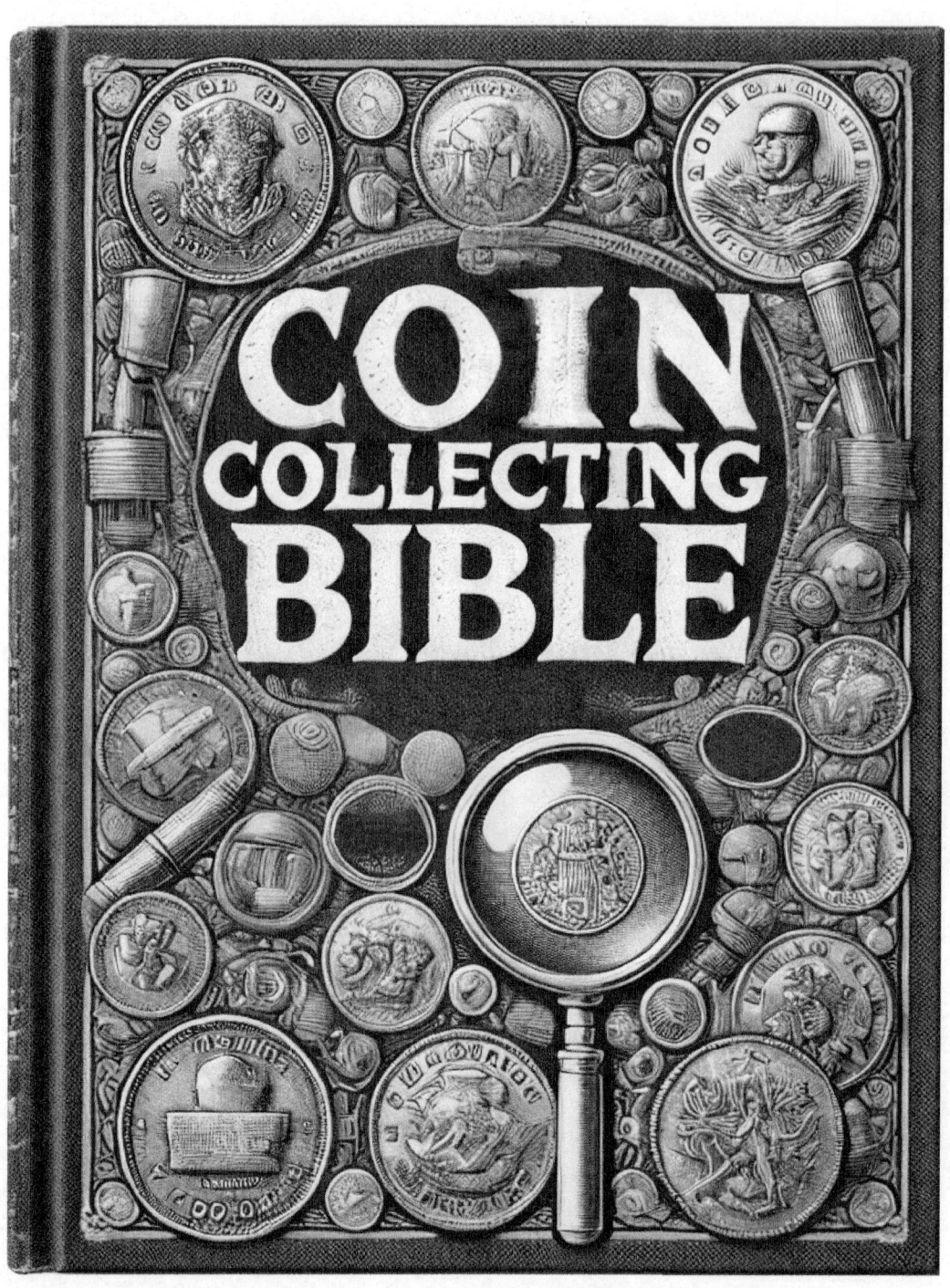

Chapter 1: Collecting Strategies

Themes and Specialties

Coin collecting, also known as numismatics, offers enthusiasts a plethora of collecting strategies centered around themes and specialties. These strategies not only cater to personal interests but also provide opportunities for in-depth exploration of historical, cultural, and artistic aspects embodied in coins. Here, we delve deeper into various themes and specialties that collectors often pursue:

1. Historical Periods and Civilizations

Definition:

- **Collecting coins based on historical periods** involves focusing on coins minted during specific eras or civilizations. This approach allows collectors to trace the evolution of coinage and historical events through numismatic artifacts.

Examples:

- **Ancient Coins:** Collecting coins from ancient civilizations such as Greek, Roman, Byzantine, Egyptian, or Chinese dynasties. Ancient coins offer insights into trade routes, cultural exchanges, and technological advancements of their times.

- **Medieval and Renaissance Coins:** Coins minted during the Middle Ages and Renaissance periods reflect the economic, political, and cultural changes in Europe and beyond. Collectors may focus on medieval kingdoms, Renaissance city-states, or religious coinage.

Benefits: Collecting by historical periods provides a comprehensive view of how coinage evolved alongside civilizations, offering tangible connections to significant historical events and societal developments.

2. Geographic Regions

Definition:

- **Geographically themed collecting** involves acquiring coins originating from specific regions or countries. This approach highlights regional histories, cultural diversity, and economic influences reflected in coin designs.

Examples:

- **National Collections:** Building collections focused on coins from a particular country, such as US coins from different states, Canadian coins, or coins from European nations like France, Germany, or Italy.

- **World Coins:** Collecting coins from various countries worldwide, showcasing the global diversity of numismatic designs, historical figures, and cultural motifs.

Benefits: Geographic collecting allows for exploration of different minting traditions, art styles, and historical narratives unique to each region, offering a global perspective within numismatics.

3. Coin Types and Denominations

Definition:

- **Collecting based on coin types and denominations** involves acquiring coins categorized by their monetary value, composition, or specific design characteristics.

Examples:

- **Series Collections:** Collecting complete sets or series of coins within a specific denomination or type, such as US Morgan Dollars, British Sovereigns, or commemorative coins issued by a particular mint.

- **Metallic Content:** Focusing on coins made from specific metals like gold, silver, or copper, which may include bullion coins, commemorative issues, or ancient coinage.

Benefits: Collecting by coin types provides a structured approach to assembling comprehensive sets, tracking design evolution, and appreciating the technical aspects of minting and metal composition.

4. Thematic and Artistic Features

Definition:

- **Thematic collecting** emphasizes coins based on specific themes or artistic motifs depicted on the coinage. This approach explores symbolism, cultural heritage, and artistic expressions through numismatic artifacts.

Examples:

- **Nature and Wildlife:** Collecting coins featuring flora, fauna, natural landscapes, or endangered species, highlighting biodiversity and environmental conservation efforts.

- **Historical Figures and Events:** Acquiring coins portraying famous leaders, influential figures, pivotal battles, or significant historical events, offering insights into political and social narratives.

Benefits: Thematic collecting allows collectors to focus on personal interests, aesthetic preferences, or thematic connections that resonate with broader historical and cultural contexts represented on coins.

5. Error Coins and Varieties

Definition:

- **Error coins and varieties collecting** focuses on coins with production errors, anomalies, or distinctive characteristics that differentiate them from standard issues.

Examples:

- **Mint Errors:** Collecting coins with striking errors such as double strikes, off-center strikes, planchet flaws, or die cracks, which add rarity and uniqueness to a collection.

- **Die Varieties:** Acquiring coins featuring variations in mint marks, die states, or design modifications that create distinct subtypes within a series.

Benefits: Error and variety collecting appeals to collectors interested in numismatic anomalies, diagnostics of minting processes, and the rarity associated with unique coin specimens.

6. Commemorative and Special-Issue Coins

Definition:

- **Collecting commemorative and special-issue coins** involves acquiring coins issued to mark significant events, anniversaries, or cultural celebrations.

Examples:

- **Anniversary Coins:** Collecting coins commemorating historical anniversaries, national milestones, or centennial celebrations, reflecting national pride and historical remembrance.

- **Thematic Issues:** Acquiring coins featuring themes such as space exploration, sports events like the Olympics, or cultural festivals, showcasing global achievements and cultural diversity.

Benefits: Commemorative collecting captures ephemeral moments in history, celebrating achievements, cultural heritage, and societal values through numismatic tributes.

7. Investment and Bullion Coins

Definition:

- **Investment-focused collecting** centers on acquiring coins for their intrinsic metal value, potential appreciation, and portfolio diversification.

Examples:

- **Gold and Silver Bullion:** Collecting coins minted from precious metals like gold or silver, valued for their purity, weight, and investment appeal in times of economic uncertainty.

- **Numismatic Investments:** Acquiring coins with historical significance, rarity, or strong collector demand, aiming for potential long-term appreciation in value due to numismatic interest and market trends.

Benefits: Investment collecting offers potential financial benefits while allowing collectors to appreciate the aesthetic, historical, and monetary aspects of numismatic assets.

Numismatics offers a wide array of collecting strategies, each providing unique insights into historical, cultural, and artistic narratives through coins. Whether collecting by historical periods, geographic regions, thematic motifs, error coins, commemorative issues, or for investment purposes, collectors engage in a journey that combines passion, knowledge, and appreciation for the diverse world of coinage. By exploring these themes and specialties, collectors enrich their understanding of global history, artistry, and economic dynamics while building meaningful and valuable collections that contribute to preserving and celebrating the heritage encapsulated in numismatic treasures.

Chapter 2: Investment considerations.

Investing in coins can be both a rewarding hobby and a strategic financial decision. Numismatic investments offer collectors and investors opportunities to diversify their portfolios, preserve wealth, and potentially generate returns over time. Here are several key investment considerations to keep in mind when entering the world of numismatics:

Investment Considerations in Numismatics

1. Historical Performance and Market Trends

- **Long-Term Appreciation:** Historically, rare coins have shown the potential for appreciation over extended periods. Coins with limited mintage, historical significance, or cultural appeal often gain value as demand from collectors increases.

- **Market Cycles:** Understanding market cycles in numismatics is crucial. Prices of coins can fluctuate based on economic conditions, collector trends, and global events. Studying historical data and consulting with experts can help anticipate market movements.

2. Quality and Rarity

- **Condition Matters:** Coins in exceptional condition (high grades) typically command higher prices due to their scarcity and appeal to collectors seeking the finest specimens.

- **Rarity:** Coins with low mintage figures, limited surviving examples, or those featuring unique attributes (such as errors or varieties) are often more sought after and can appreciate significantly over time.

3. Authentication and Provenance

- **Authenticity:** Ensuring the authenticity of coins is paramount. Working with reputable dealers, obtaining certification from recognized grading services (e.g., NGC, PCGS), and verifying provenance (history of ownership) can mitigate risks associated with counterfeit or altered coins.

- **Documentation:** Maintain thorough documentation of purchase receipts, certificates of authenticity, and grading reports to validate the coin's provenance and quality.

4. Diversification and Portfolio Allocation

- **Portfolio Diversification:** Including numismatic assets in a diversified investment portfolio can provide stability and hedge against volatility in traditional financial markets.

- **Risk Management:** Allocate a portion of investment capital to numismatics based on individual risk tolerance, financial goals, and the liquidity needs of the overall portfolio.

5. Market Liquidity and Exit Strategies

- **Liquidity Considerations:** Numismatic investments can vary in liquidity. Highly desirable coins may be easier to sell quickly at favorable prices, while niche or less liquid segments of the market may require longer holding periods.

- **Exit Strategies:** Have clear exit strategies in place. Whether selling through auctions, private sales, or specialized dealers, understanding market conditions and timing can optimize returns on investment.

6. Educational Resources and Expert Advice

- **Continuous Learning:** Stay informed about numismatic trends, market developments, and historical contexts through publications, online resources, and participation in numismatic communities.

- **Consultation:** Seek advice from numismatic experts, financial advisors specializing in alternative investments, and reputable dealers to make informed decisions aligned with investment objectives.

7. Personal Enjoyment and Passion

- **Collecting vs. Investing:** Balance financial considerations with personal enjoyment. Numismatics offers the opportunity to appreciate history, artistry, and culture through collecting coins that resonate personally.

- **Legacy Planning:** Consider numismatic assets in estate planning to preserve collections for future generations or charitable purposes, leveraging potential tax benefits and ensuring continuity of passion-driven investments.

Investing in coins requires careful consideration of historical performance, market dynamics, quality, authenticity, and personal objectives. Numismatic investments can offer diversification benefits, potential appreciation, and the satisfaction of collecting tangible pieces of history and culture. By understanding these investment considerations and conducting thorough research, collectors and investors can navigate the nuances of numismatics effectively, making informed decisions that align with their financial goals and personal interests.

Chapter 3: Profiles of notable collectors.

Profiles of notable collectors in the field of numismatics provide insight into their passion, contributions to the hobby, and the impact they have had on preserving and expanding knowledge of coin collecting. Here are profiles of a few renowned collectors:

Profiles of Notable Numismatic Collectors

1. Louis E. Eliasberg Sr. (1896-1976)

Background:

- **Legacy:** Louis Eliasberg is celebrated as the only individual to assemble a complete collection of United States coins by date and mintmark. His collection, known as the "Eliasberg Collection," comprised nearly every coin ever minted by the United States from 1792 to the mid-20th century.

- **Achievements:** Eliasberg's dedication to completeness and quality set a standard in numismatics. His collection included rare coins such as the 1913 Liberty Head nickel and all three types of 1804 silver dollars.

2. John Jay Pittman (1913-1996)

Background:

- **Collector and Philanthropist:** John Jay Pittman was a prominent figure in numismatics renowned for his extensive collection of American and world coins. He started collecting as a child and continued throughout his life, amassing a collection that included over 20,000 coins.

- **Legacy:** Pittman's collection was notable for its breadth and quality, featuring rare coins such as the 1804 Draped Bust dollar and the 1913 Liberty Head nickel. After his passing, his collection was auctioned by David Akers and became known as the "Pittman Collection," contributing significantly to numismatic scholarship and availability of rare coins in the market.

3. King Farouk of Egypt (1920-1965)

Background:

- **Royal Collector:** King Farouk of Egypt was a passionate and prolific collector of coins, amassing one of the most extensive and valuable collections in the world during his reign from 1936 to 1952.

- **Collection:** Farouk's collection included coins spanning ancient civilizations to contemporary issues, featuring rarities from Egypt, Europe, and beyond. His collection was known for its exceptional quality and historical significance.

- **Impact:** After his deposition in 1952, Farouk's collection was dispersed through auctions, influencing the availability and appreciation of numismatic treasures globally.

4. Harry W. Bass Jr. (1927-1998)

Background:

- **Researcher and Collector:** Harry Bass Jr. was a dedicated numismatist known for his focus on U.S. pattern coins and early American coppers. He meticulously researched and cataloged his collection, contributing significantly to the understanding of these coin types.

- **Legacy:** The Harry W. Bass Jr. Collection, particularly his extensive holdings of pattern coins, remains a cornerstone of numismatic research and study. His collection was donated to the American Numismatic Association (ANA) and is housed in the ANA Money Museum.

5. D. Brent Pogue (1962-2019)

Background:

- **Modern Collector:** Brent Pogue gained renown for assembling one of the most valuable collections of early American coins and currency, focusing on quality and rarity.

- **Achievements:** Pogue's collection included legendary coins such as the 1804 Draped Bust dollar and the finest known 1822 Capped Head Left half eagle.

His auctions, conducted by Stack's Bowers Galleries and Sotheby's, set numerous records in the numismatic world.

Impact and Contributions

These collectors have left lasting legacies in the field of numismatics through their passion, dedication to quality, and contributions to scholarly research. Their collections not only advanced the understanding of coinage but also enriched the hobby by making rare and historically significant coins accessible to future generations through public exhibitions and auctions. Their profiles inspire collectors and enthusiasts alike to pursue excellence in collecting, preservation, and the appreciation of numismatic treasures worldwide.

Famous coin collections and their histories.

Exploring famous coin collections offers a glimpse into the passion, dedication, and historical significance associated with these treasured assemblies of numismatic artifacts. Here are profiles of some renowned coin collections and their histories:

Famous Coin Collections and Their Histories

1. The Eliasberg Collection

Collector: Louis E. Eliasberg Sr. (1896-1976)

Overview:

- **Scope:** The Eliasberg Collection is widely regarded as one of the most complete and significant collections of United States coins ever assembled.

- **Achievements:** Louis Eliasberg achieved the remarkable feat of acquiring at least one example of every regular-issue United States coin from 1793 to 1954, including major rarities like the 1913 Liberty Head nickel and all three types of 1804 silver dollars.

- **Legacy:** After Eliasberg's passing, the collection was sold in a series of auctions by Bowers and Merena Galleries from 1982 to 1997, dispersing its treasures to collectors and institutions worldwide.

2. The Pittman Collection

Collector: John Jay Pittman (1913-1996)

Overview:

- **Scope:** John Jay Pittman's collection encompassed a vast array of American and world coins, totaling over 20,000 pieces at its peak.

- **Highlights:** The Pittman Collection featured rare and valuable coins such as the 1804 Draped Bust dollar, multiple examples of the 1913 Liberty Head nickel, and significant European and Asian numismatic treasures.

- **Dispersal:** Following Pittman's death, his collection was auctioned by David Akers from 1997 to 1999, becoming known as the "Pittman Collection" and contributing substantially to numismatic scholarship and the availability of rare coins in the market.

3. The King Farouk Collection

Collector: King Farouk of Egypt (1920-1965)

Overview:

- **Royal Collection:** King Farouk was a passionate collector who amassed one of the most extensive and valuable collections of coins during his reign.

- **Contents:** The Farouk Collection included ancient coins, Islamic coins, European rarities, and exceptional examples of Egyptian numismatic history.

- **Auction and Dispersal:** Following King Farouk's deposition in 1952, his collection was auctioned by Sotheby's in Cairo, marking one of the most significant numismatic events of the 20th century. The dispersal of the Farouk Collection introduced many rare coins to the international market.

4. The Harry W. Bass Jr. Collection

Collector: Harry W. Bass Jr. (1927-1998)

Overview:

- **Focus:** Harry Bass Jr. specialized in collecting U.S. pattern coins and early American coppers, focusing on research and cataloging.

- **Legacy:** His collection, known as the Harry W. Bass Jr. Collection, became renowned for its comprehensive holdings and meticulous documentation.

- **Donation:** Upon his passing, the collection was donated to the American Numismatic Association (ANA) and is housed in the ANA Money Museum, serving as a valuable educational resource for scholars, collectors, and enthusiasts.

5. The D. Brent Pogue Collection

Collector: D. Brent Pogue (1962-2019)

Overview:

- **Notability:** Brent Pogue gained fame for assembling one of the most valuable collections of early American coins and currency, emphasizing quality and rarity.

- **Achievements:** The Pogue Collection featured iconic coins such as the 1804 Draped Bust dollar, the finest known 1822 Capped Head Left half eagle, and numerous other rarities.

- **Auctions:** Pogue's collection was auctioned in a series of sales by Stack's Bowers Galleries and Sotheby's from 2015 to 2021, setting records for individual coin prices and generating significant interest in numismatic circles.

Impact and Legacy

These famous coin collections not only exemplify the passion and dedication of their collectors but also enrich numismatic scholarship, public exhibitions, and the broader appreciation of coins as historical artifacts. Through their dispersal via auctions or donations to institutions, these collections continue to inspire collectors and enthusiasts worldwide, preserving the legacy of numismatic treasures for future generations to admire and study.

Auctions in the numismatic world often make headlines for record-breaking sales, showcasing rare and historically significant coins that capture the imagination of collectors and investors alike. Here are some auction highlights and record-breaking sales that have left a lasting mark in numismatic history:

Chapter 4: Auction Highlights and Record-Breaking Sales

1. The 1804 Draped Bust Silver Dollar

- **Highlights:** The 1804 Draped Bust dollar is one of the most famous and valuable coins in American numismatics, despite not actually being minted in 1804. Only 15 examples are known to exist, and each has a fascinating history.

- **Record Sale:** In August 1999, the finest known Class I (original) 1804 Draped Bust dollar, previously owned by the Sultan of Muscat, was sold at a public auction by Bowers and Merena Galleries for $4.14 million. This sale set a record for the highest price ever paid for a single coin at auction at the time.

2. The 1933 Double Eagle

- **Highlights:** The 1933 Double Eagle is another legendary coin in American numismatics. Although the U.S. Mint never officially released any 1933 Double Eagles for circulation due to changes in gold ownership laws during the Great Depression, a few specimens were illegally removed from the Mint.

- **Record Sale:** In 2002, a 1933 Double Eagle was sold by Sotheby's and Stack's for $7.59 million, setting a record for the highest price ever paid for a single coin at auction at that time. This sale highlighted the rarity and allure of the 1933 Double Eagle in the numismatic market.

3. The 1913 Liberty Head Nickel

- **Highlights:** The 1913 Liberty Head nickel is one of the most famous and enigmatic coins in American numismatics. Only five examples are known to exist, and they were clandestinely struck under mysterious circumstances.

- **Record Sale:** In January 2014, one of the five known 1913 Liberty Head nickels, previously owned by a collector, was sold by Heritage Auctions for $3.29 million. This sale marked a significant achievement in numismatic history and demonstrated the enduring appeal of this rare coin.

4. The 1794 Flowing Hair Silver Dollar

- **Highlights:** The 1794 Flowing Hair silver dollar holds the distinction of being the first dollar coin issued by the United States Mint. It is a symbol of American numismatic heritage and the young nation's aspirations.

- **Record Sale:** In January 2013, Stack's Bowers Galleries sold a specimen of the 1794 Flowing Hair silver dollar for $10 million, setting a record for the highest price ever paid for a single coin at auction. This sale underscored the historical significance and rarity of early American coinage.

5. The Brasher Doubloon

- **Highlights:** The Brasher Doubloon is one of the earliest gold coins struck in the United States and is revered for its historical importance and craftsmanship. It was minted by New York goldsmith Ephraim Brasher in 1787.

- **Record Sale:** In December 2011, a Brasher Doubloon, the EB on Wing variety, was sold by Heritage Auctions for $7.4 million. This sale set a record for the highest price ever paid for a pre-Federal American coin at auction, highlighting its significance in American numismatics.

Impact and Significance

These auction highlights and record-breaking sales not only reflect the rarity and historical importance of these coins but also demonstrate the strong demand and passion within the numismatic community. Each sale sets new benchmarks in the valuation of numismatic treasures, attracting collectors, investors, and enthusiasts eager to own a piece of history. These auctions continue to shape the landscape of coin collecting, preserving and promoting the appreciation of numismatic heritage for future generations.

BOOK 8

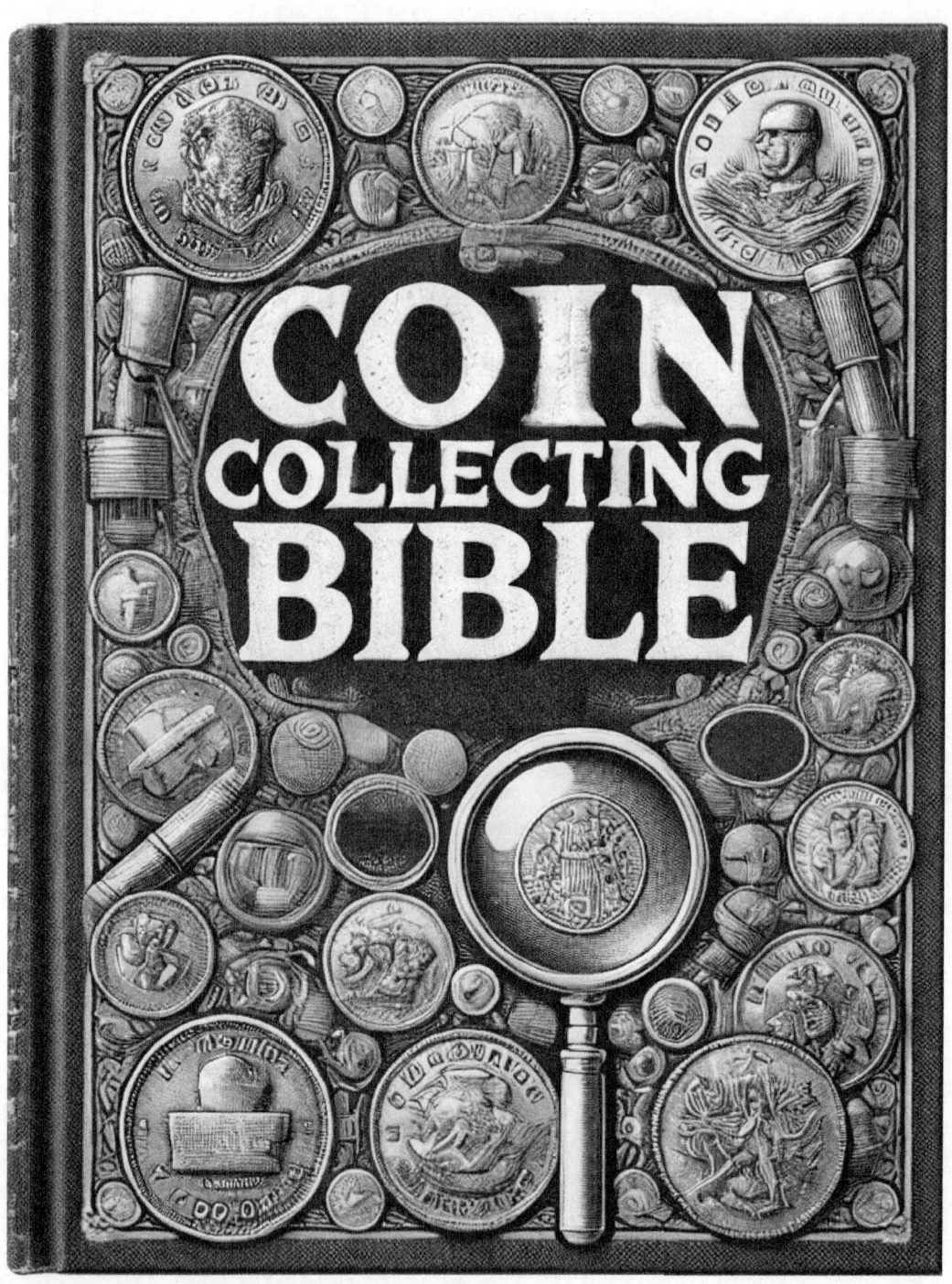

Chapter 1: Storage and Preservation of Coins

Proper storage and preservation are critical to maintaining the condition and value of coin collections over time. Whether you're a seasoned collector or new to numismatics, understanding the best practices for handling and storing coins is essential. Here's a comprehensive guide to help you preserve your coin collection:

1. Handling Practices

- **Clean Hands:** Always wash and dry your hands thoroughly before handling coins to avoid transferring oils, dirt, or moisture.

- **Use Gloves:** For particularly valuable or delicate coins, wear soft cotton or nitrile gloves to prevent direct contact.

- **Handle by Edges:** Hold coins by the edges rather than touching the surfaces, as fingerprints and abrasions can affect their condition.

- **Avoid Cleaning:** Refrain from cleaning coins unless absolutely necessary and under expert guidance, as improper cleaning can damage their surfaces and diminish their value.

2. Storage Environment

- **Stable Temperature and Humidity:** Store coins in a stable environment with moderate temperature (ideally 65-75°F) and humidity (around 50-55% RH) to prevent corrosion and damage.

- **Avoid Extremes:** Keep coins away from direct sunlight, extreme heat, cold, and fluctuating humidity, as these can accelerate deterioration.

- **Use Encapsulated Holders:** Store individual coins in archival-quality, inert holders such as coin flips, Mylar sleeves, or 2x2 cardboard holders to protect them from environmental contaminants.

3. Long-Term Storage Solutions

- **Albums and Folders:** Use numismatic albums with acid-free pages and PVC-free plastic sleeves for organizing and displaying coin collections.

- **Coin Trays and Boxes:** Store coins in designated coin trays or boxes made from archival materials, ensuring they are properly labeled and organized.

- **Safe Deposit Box:** For high-value or irreplaceable coins, consider storing them in a bank's safe deposit box to provide added security and protection.

4. Avoid Chemicals and Abrasives

- **Cleaning Products:** Never use abrasive materials, household cleaners, or chemicals to clean coins. If cleaning is necessary, use distilled water or mild soap with guidance from a professional conservator.

- **Storage Materials:** Choose storage materials that are free of PVC, which can emit harmful gases and damage coins over time.

5. Regular Inspection and Maintenance

- **Inspect Periodically:** Check your coin collection regularly for signs of damage, discoloration, or pests. Address any issues promptly to prevent further deterioration.

- **Rotate Display:** If displaying coins, rotate them periodically to minimize exposure to light and handling.

6. Insurance and Documentation

- **Insurance Coverage:** Consider insuring your coin collection against theft, loss, or damage. Keep updated inventory records, including photographs and descriptions, for insurance purposes.

- **Documentation:** Maintain detailed records of acquisition, provenance, and any professional certifications or appraisals to establish authenticity and value.

7. Professional Conservation

- **Conservation Services:** Consult professional conservators or numismatic experts for conservation treatments if coins require specialized care or restoration.

- **Restoration:** Avoid amateur attempts at coin restoration, as improper techniques can irreversibly damage coins.

By following these guidelines for proper handling, storage, and preservation, you can protect the integrity and value of your coin collection for years to come. Remember that each coin is a unique piece of history deserving of careful stewardship. Investing in quality storage materials and maintaining a stable environment will ensure that your coins remain in excellent condition, preserving their beauty and historical significance for future generations of collectors to appreciate.

Chapter 2: Storage Methods for Coin Collections

Proper storage is essential for preserving the condition and value of coin collections. Different storage methods cater to various needs, from organization and display to long-term preservation. Here are effective storage methods commonly used by collectors:

1. Coin Albums

- **Description:** Coin albums are binders with pages designed to hold coins in individual slots, typically made of cardboard or plastic.

- **Advantages:**

  o Organize coins by type, date, or theme.

  o Provide easy viewing and access to each coin.

  o Protect coins from dust and light exposure.

- **Considerations:**

- o Choose albums with acid-free pages and PVC-free materials to prevent chemical damage.

- o Ensure pages are sturdy to support the weight of coins without causing damage.

2. Coin Holders (Flips or 2x2s)

- **Description:** Coin holders are small, clear, plastic sleeves or envelopes that encapsulate individual coins.

- **Advantages:**

  - o Protect coins from physical damage and environmental contaminants.

  - o Allow easy handling and inspection without direct contact.

  - o Ideal for storage in coin trays, boxes, or albums.

- **Considerations:**

  - o Use holders made of archival-quality materials to prevent PVC damage.

  - o Label holders with coin information and avoid excessive handling to minimize wear.

3. Coin Cases and Display Boxes

- **Description:** Coin cases are durable containers made of plastic, wood, or metal, designed to hold multiple coins securely.

- **Advantages:**

  - o Provides protection against moisture, dust, and physical impact.

- o Offer options for organizing and displaying coins attractively.

- o Suitable for showcasing valuable or thematic collections.

- **Considerations:**

  - o Choose cases with compartments or trays that fit coin sizes snugly to prevent movement.

  - o Ensure materials are non-reactive and do not emit harmful gases that could damage coins.

4. Coin Tubes and Rolls

- **Description:** Coin tubes are cylindrical containers made of clear plastic or cardboard, designed to store and transport large quantities of coins.

- **Advantages:**

  - o Efficient storage solution for bulk coins, such as mint rolls or loose change.

  - o Protect coins from scratches and abrasions.

  - o Stackable and easy to store in safes or vaults.

- **Considerations:**

  - o Label tubes with coin denominations or types for easy identification.

  - o Use tubes that are free from oils or residues that could transfer to coins.

5. Safe Deposit Boxes

- **Description:** Safe deposit boxes are secure storage units provided by banks or financial institutions.

- **Advantages:**

  o Maximum security against theft, fire, and environmental damage.

  o Ideal for storing high-value or irreplaceable coins.

  o Peace of mind with insurance coverage options.

- **Considerations:**

  o Choose a reputable bank with a climate-controlled facility to prevent humidity damage.

  o Keep an updated inventory of contents for insurance purposes.

Choosing the Right Storage Method

- **Assess Your Collection:** Consider the size, value, and organization needs of your coin collection.

- **Prioritize Protection:** Select storage methods that provide adequate protection against environmental factors, physical damage, and handling.

- **Quality Materials:** Invest in archival-quality materials that are inert and non-reactive to ensure long-term preservation.

- **Regular Maintenance:** Inspect and maintain your storage solutions periodically to prevent deterioration and ensure coins remain in optimal condition.

By employing appropriate storage methods tailored to your collection's needs, you can safeguard the integrity and longevity of your coins while enjoying the beauty and historical significance they represent.

Chapter 3: Protection Against Oxidation (Toning or Tarnishing)

Understanding Oxidation:

Oxidation occurs when metals in coins react with elements in the environment, such as oxygen, moisture, or sulfur compounds. This reaction can result in toning or tarnishing, altering the appearance of the coin's surface. While toning is natural and can sometimes enhance a coin's beauty, severe oxidation can diminish its aesthetic appeal and market value if not properly managed.

Preventive Measures:

1. **Proper Storage Environment:**

   o **Stable Conditions:** Maintain a stable environment with controlled temperature and humidity. Fluctuations in these conditions can accelerate oxidation. Ideal storage conditions are typically around 65-75°F (18-24°C) and 50-55% relative humidity.

   o **Air-Tight Containers:** Store coins in air-tight containers such as capsules or holders to minimize exposure to air and moisture. Choose holders made from materials that do not contain PVC (Polyvinyl Chloride), as PVC can emit harmful gases that accelerate toning.

- o **Desiccants:** Include silica gel packets or other desiccants in storage containers to absorb any moisture that might be present.

2. **Avoiding Contaminants:**

- o **Avoid Handling:** Limit handling of coins, as oils and residues from fingers can transfer to the coin's surface and accelerate toning.

- o **Clean Environment:** Store coins in a clean environment free from pollutants that can contribute to oxidation. Dust and pollutants can settle on coins and react with their surfaces over time.

3. **Interleaving and Separation:**

- o **Interleaving:** Place acid-free paper or Mylar between coins in storage to prevent them from touching each other. This reduces the risk of toning transfer between coins.

- o **Individual Storage:** Store each coin separately to prevent contact with other metals or materials that may accelerate oxidation.

4. **Monitoring and Maintenance:**

- o **Regular Inspection:** Periodically inspect coins for signs of toning or tarnishing. Early detection allows for timely intervention to prevent further oxidation.

o **Conservation Guidance:** Consult with professional numismatists or conservators for advice on handling and preserving coins, especially if you notice signs of advanced toning or tarnishing.

Protection Against Scratches and Physical Damage

Causes of Scratches:

Scratches on coins can occur due to mishandling, improper storage, or contact with abrasive surfaces. Even minor scratches can affect a coin's grade and aesthetic appeal, potentially reducing its value.

Preventive Measures:

1. **Handling Techniques:**

   o **Use Gloves:** Wear soft cotton or nitrile gloves when handling coins to minimize the risk of transferring oils or causing scratches with bare hands.

   o **Hold by Edges:** Handle coins by the edges rather than touching the surfaces. This reduces the risk of leaving fingerprints or scratches on the coin's face.

2. **Storage Practices:**

   o **Soft Surfaces:** When examining or displaying coins, use soft padded surfaces such as felt or microfiber cloths to cushion the coin and minimize the risk of accidental drops or impacts.

o **Individual Holders:** Store coins individually in holders, capsules, or flips made from inert materials to protect them from scratches caused by contact with other coins or storage materials.

3. **Avoid Cleaning:**

   o **Gentle Handling:** Refrain from cleaning coins unnecessarily. Abrasive cleaning methods or harsh chemicals can cause scratches and irreparably damage the coin's surface.

   o **Professional Guidance:** If cleaning is necessary, seek advice from professional conservators who specialize in numismatic conservation to ensure proper techniques are used.

By implementing these comprehensive strategies for protecting coins against oxidation and scratches, collectors can safeguard their collections' beauty, historical integrity, and monetary value. Consistent attention to proper storage, handling practices, and environmental conditions ensures that coins retain their pristine condition and remain a source of pride and enjoyment for generations to come. Investing in quality storage materials and consulting with experts when needed are invaluable steps toward preserving numismatic treasures for the future.

BOOK 9

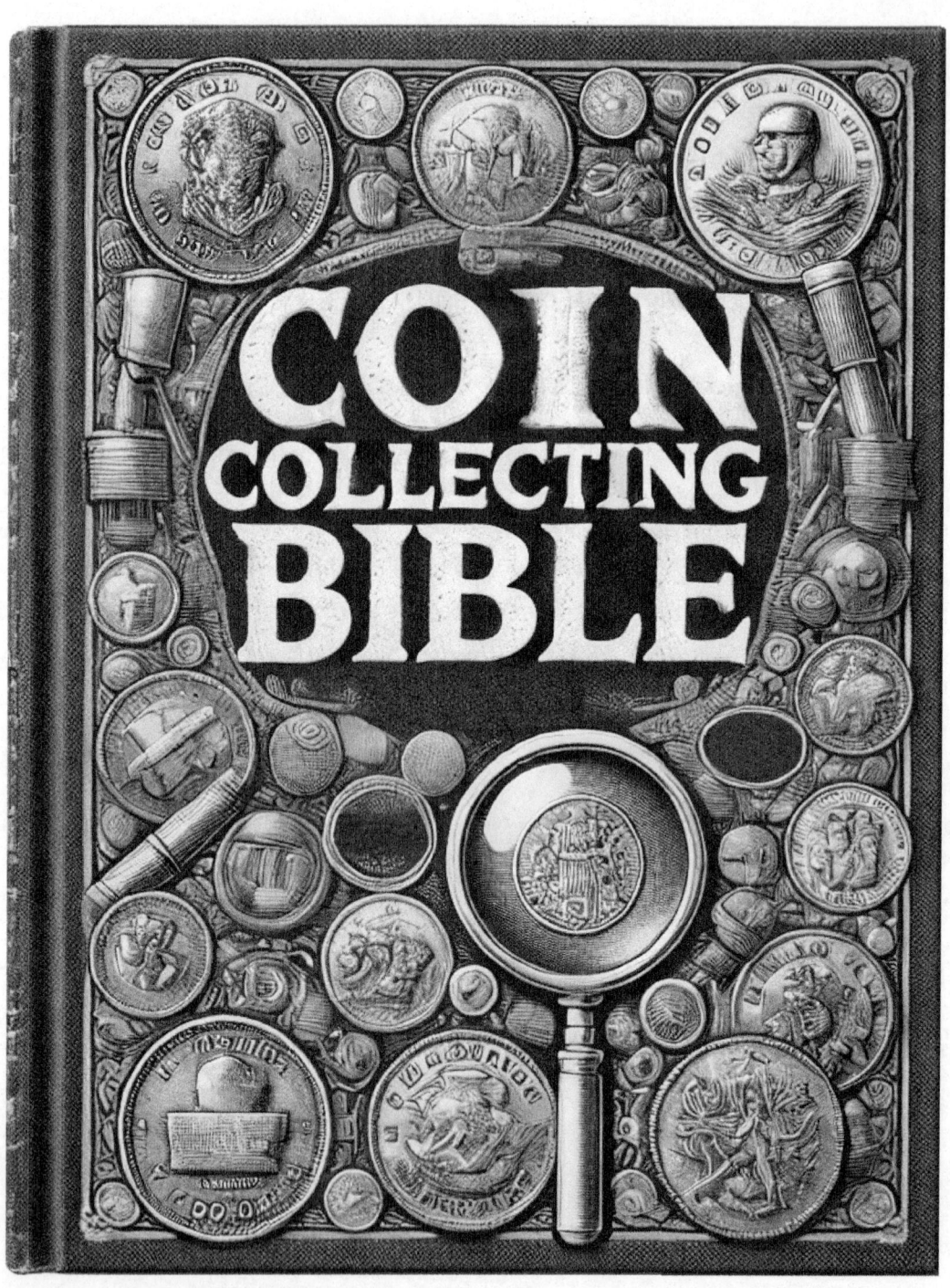

Chapter 1: Numismatic Technology

Coin Authentication Techniques

In the world of numismatics, ensuring the authenticity of coins is paramount. Over the years, advancements in technology have revolutionized the methods used to authenticate coins, providing collectors, dealers, and museums with sophisticated tools to verify the genuineness of numismatic artifacts. Here are some key coin authentication techniques widely used today:

1. Traditional Methods

- **Visual Inspection:** Experienced numismatists often rely on visual inspection to detect signs of counterfeiting or alterations. They examine details such as design elements, lettering, and mint marks for inconsistencies or anomalies.

- **Weight and Diameter:** Comparing a coin's weight and diameter to standard specifications can indicate authenticity. Counterfeit coins often deviate from these measurements due to differences in materials or manufacturing techniques.

- **Metal Composition:** Analyzing the metal composition using X-ray fluorescence (XRF) or other spectroscopic methods helps determine if the coin's composition matches known authentic examples.

2. Advanced Authentication Techniques

- **Microscopic Examination:** High-resolution microscopes and digital imaging technologies allow experts to examine coins at magnifications that reveal minute details, including tool marks and surface characteristics that are difficult to replicate.

- **Edge Lettering and Reeding:** Examination of edge lettering and reeding (if present) under magnification can reveal signs of casting or machining that are indicative of counterfeit production methods.

- **X-ray Imaging:** X-ray imaging techniques, such as X-ray radiography, are used to inspect the interior structure of coins without damaging them. This method can reveal hidden features or discrepancies in internal composition.

- **Ultraviolet (UV) Light:** UV light examination can highlight differences in fluorescence or phosphorescence between genuine and counterfeit coins, as some materials used in counterfeiting may react differently under UV illumination.

3. Technological Innovations

- **Computerized Image Analysis:** Software programs designed for coin authentication analyze digital images of coins to compare them against a database of known authentic examples. These programs can detect subtle differences in design, relief, and surface characteristics.

- **Laser Technology:** Laser scanning and spectroscopy techniques are employed to analyze surface topography and chemical composition, providing detailed data on a coin's authenticity and condition.

- **Blockchain Technology:** Emerging in the numismatic world, blockchain technology is used to create secure digital records of coin ownership, provenance, and authenticity, enhancing transparency and traceability in the marketplace.

4. Certification and Grading Services

- **Professional Authentication Services:** Numismatic authentication is often conducted by reputable grading services, such as Numismatic Guaranty Corporation (NGC), Professional Coin Grading Service (PCGS), and others. These services employ a combination of traditional and advanced techniques to authenticate and grade coins.

- **Certification Labels and Seals:** Authenticated coins are encapsulated in tamper-evident holders with certification labels and seals, providing assurance of authenticity and grade to buyers and sellers in the numismatic market.

Chapter 2: Digital Tools for Numismatic Collectors

In the digital age, numismatic collectors have access to a wealth of resources and tools that enhance their hobby, from managing collections to researching and authenticating coins. Here are some popular digital tools, apps, and databases that cater to numismatic enthusiasts:

1. Numismatic Apps

- **Coin Catalog Apps:** These apps provide extensive databases of coins from around the world, allowing collectors to catalog and organize their collections digitally. Examples include:

  - **PCGS CoinFacts:** Provides information and images of coins with details on varieties, grades, and market values.

  - **NGC Coin Explorer:** Offers a comprehensive database of coins, including historical background, grading details, and pricing information.

  - **Coinoscope:** Allows users to identify coins by uploading photos and provides information on the coin's origin, history, and characteristics.

2. Auction Platforms

- **Online Auctions:** Platforms like Heritage Auctions, Stack's Bowers Galleries, and eBay facilitate buying and selling of coins, offering a wide range of numismatic items from ancient to modern times. Collectors can participate in auctions, track prices, and add desired coins to their collections.

3. Digital Coin Catalogs

- **Online Databases:** Websites such as Numista, CoinWeek, and NumisMaster provide comprehensive catalogs of coins with images, descriptions, and historical details. Collectors can use these resources for research, identification, and cataloging their collections.

4. Grading and Authentication Tools

- **PCGS Cert Verification:** The PCGS Certification Verification tool allows users to verify the authenticity and grade of PCGS-certified coins by entering the certification number. It provides detailed information about the coin's grade, pedigree, and population.

- **NGC Certification Verification:** Similar to PCGS, the NGC Certification Verification tool verifies the authenticity and grade of NGC-certified coins and provides relevant information and population data.

5. Coin Inventory Management

- **Collector's Edge:** This app allows collectors to manage their coin collections by organizing coins into categories, tracking purchase history, setting goals, and generating reports on collection value and inventory.

- **CoinManage:** Software for Windows that helps collectors organize, manage, and track their coin collections. It includes a comprehensive database of coins with images and detailed information for cataloging purposes.

6. Research and Education

- **Online Forums and Communities:** Platforms like Reddit's r/coins, CoinTalk Forum, and Collector's Universe provide spaces for collectors to discuss coins, share knowledge, seek advice, and engage with other enthusiasts.

- **Educational Websites:** Websites like American Numismatic Association (ANA), British Numismatic Society (BNS), and Royal Numismatic Society

(RNS) offer educational resources, articles, and publications on numismatics, history, and coin collecting.

Benefits of Digital Tools for Numismatic Collectors

- **Accessibility:** Instant access to vast databases of coins, pricing information, and historical context.

- **Organization:** Simplified cataloging and management of coin collections with digital tools and apps.

- **Research:** Enhanced research capabilities for identifying coins, learning about their history, and understanding market trends.

- **Authentication:** Tools for verifying the authenticity and certification details of coins from reputable grading services.

Advances in coin analysis and conservation.

Advances in coin analysis and conservation have significantly evolved, employing cutting-edge technologies and methodologies that enhance the understanding, preservation, and authentication of numismatic artifacts. These advancements have revolutionized the field of numismatics, offering collectors, museums, and researchers sophisticated tools to study, protect, and maintain coin collections. Here are key areas where advances have made a substantial impact:

Advances in Coin Analysis

1. Imaging Technologies

- **High-Resolution Digital Imaging:** Modern digital cameras and microscopes equipped with high-resolution sensors capture detailed images of coins, revealing surface features, minting errors, and subtle variations that aid in identification and authentication.

- **Three-Dimensional Scanning:** Techniques like laser scanning and photogrammetry create precise 3D models of coins, allowing for detailed analysis of relief, design elements, and surface characteristics without physical contact.

2. Spectroscopic Techniques

- **X-ray Fluorescence (XRF):** XRF analysis identifies the elemental composition of coins by measuring the characteristic X-ray emissions produced when the coin is irradiated. This technique helps verify metal content and detect counterfeit materials.

- **Raman Spectroscopy:** Raman spectroscopy analyzes the molecular composition of materials on the coin's surface. It identifies pigments, corrosion products, and residues that provide insights into manufacturing techniques and environmental exposure.

3. Surface Topography and Wear Analysis

- **White-Light Interferometry:** This non-destructive technique measures surface roughness and wear patterns on coins at a microscopic level. It helps determine circulation wear, distinguish genuine wear from artificial aging, and assess preservation conditions.

4. Chemical Analysis

- **Mass Spectrometry:** Mass spectrometry identifies and quantifies trace elements and isotopes in coins, offering clues about their origin, minting techniques, and historical context.

Advances in Coin Conservation

1. Non-Invasive Cleaning and Preservation

- **Gentle Cleaning Techniques:** Conservationists use specialized tools and solvents to remove surface contaminants and stabilize coins without altering their original surfaces or patina.

- **Microabrasive Cleaning:** Controlled microabrasive techniques remove encrustations and stubborn deposits from coins with minimal impact on their surfaces.

2. Micro-Environmental Control

- **Microclimate Enclosures:** Advanced storage solutions provide micro-environments tailored to control temperature, humidity, and atmospheric pollutants around individual coins. This helps prevent oxidation, corrosion, and physical damage over time.

3. Protective Coatings and Treatments

- **Barrier Coatings:** Thin protective coatings such as microcrystalline wax or acrylic resins shield coins from environmental pollutants, moisture, and handling damage while maintaining their appearance.

4. Digital Documentation and Preservation

- **Digital Archives:** Digital databases and repositories store detailed records, images, and analytical data of coins. These archives facilitate long-term preservation, research access, and dissemination of numismatic knowledge.

Benefits and Implications

- **Enhanced Authentication:** Advanced analysis techniques provide more accurate methods to authenticate coins by confirming metal composition, minting characteristics, and historical authenticity.

- **Preservation of Historical Artifacts:** Conservation advancements ensure the long-term survival of numismatic artifacts, preserving their aesthetic integrity and historical significance for future generations.

- **Scientific Insights:** Coin analysis contributes to broader historical and archaeological research, shedding light on ancient economies, trade routes, and cultural exchanges through numismatic evidence.

Chapter 3: Emerging trends in numismatics.

Emerging trends in numismatics reflect shifts in collecting interests, technological advancements, market dynamics, and broader societal influences. These trends are shaping the landscape of coin collecting and influencing how collectors engage with numismatic artifacts. Here are some notable emerging trends in numismatics:

1. Focus on Diversity and Inclusivity

- **Representation in Numismatics:** There is a growing emphasis on coins that reflect diverse cultures, historical figures, and significant events previously underrepresented in mainstream collections.

- **Inclusivity:** Collectors are seeking coins that celebrate diversity in design, themes, and historical narratives, promoting inclusivity within the numismatic community.

2. Digitalization and Online Engagement

- **Digital Platforms:** The proliferation of online databases, auction platforms, and numismatic apps has facilitated easier access to information, market trends, and opportunities for collectors globally.

- **Virtual Collecting:** Increasing numbers of collectors are participating in virtual auctions, online forums, and digital exhibitions, expanding their collections and knowledge without physical attendance.

3. Technological Integration

- **Digital Tools:** Advances in imaging, spectroscopy, and database technologies are enhancing authentication, research capabilities, and conservation practices within numismatics.

- **Blockchain and Digital Ownership:** Experimentation with blockchain technology for certifying ownership, provenance, and authenticity of coins is gaining traction, offering enhanced security and transparency in transactions.

4. Environmental and Ethical Considerations

- **Sustainable Collecting:** There is a rising awareness of the environmental impact of numismatic activities. Collectors are seeking ethically sourced materials and supporting sustainable practices in coin production and conservation.

- **Cultural Heritage Protection:** Increased efforts to protect cultural heritage, combat illicit trafficking, and repatriate stolen artifacts are influencing collectors' choices and the regulation of numismatic trade.

5. Artistic Innovation and Design

- **Contemporary Coin Designs:** Mints and artists are exploring innovative design concepts, incorporating modern aesthetics, and pushing the boundaries of traditional numismatic artistry.

- **Limited Editions and Special Releases:** Collectors are drawn to limited-edition coins, special finishes, and collaborations between mints and renowned artists or designers, adding exclusivity and artistic value to collections.

6. Education and Outreach

- **Numismatic Education:** Institutions, museums, and online platforms are expanding educational programs and resources to promote numismatic literacy, attract new collectors, and engage younger audiences.

- **Community Building:** Social media platforms, virtual events, and local numismatic clubs foster community engagement, knowledge sharing, and mentorship among collectors of all ages.

7. Investment and Market Trends

- **Investment Potential:** Numismatics continues to attract investors seeking tangible assets with historical value and potential appreciation over time, influencing market demand and pricing dynamics.

- **Numismatic Investment Funds:** The emergence of investment funds specializing in rare coins and collectibles provides opportunities for institutional investors to diversify portfolios and access the numismatic market.

Market cycles and investment strategies.

Understanding market cycles and developing sound investment strategies are crucial for numismatic collectors and investors aiming to navigate the complexities of the coin market. Numismatics, like other investment sectors, experiences cycles influenced by various factors, including economic conditions, collector trends, and market sentiment. Here's an overview of market cycles and effective investment strategies in numismatics:

Market Cycles in Numismatics

1. Boom Phase

- **Characteristics:** During this phase, there is heightened demand and increasing prices for rare and desirable coins.

- **Factors:** Factors such as historical significance, rarity, and aesthetic appeal drive enthusiasm among collectors and investors.

- **Examples:** Newly discovered hoards, significant auction results, or popular coin series experiencing renewed interest can fuel the boom phase.

2. Plateau Phase

- **Characteristics:** Prices stabilize as market enthusiasm cools down from the boom phase.

- **Factors:** Market saturation for popular coins, moderate collector interest, or economic stability contribute to a balanced pricing environment.

- **Examples:** Established collector coins with steady demand and stable pricing maintain their value during this phase.

3. Bust Phase

- **Characteristics:** Prices decline as demand softens and market corrections occur.

- **Factors:** Economic downturns, changes in collector preferences, or oversupply of certain coin types contribute to price adjustments.

- **Examples:** Speculative bubbles bursting, excessive inventory flooding the market, or shifts in investor sentiment can trigger the bust phase.

Investment Strategies in Numismatics

1. Diversification

- **Spread Risk:** Diversify your numismatic portfolio across different types of coins, historical periods, and price ranges to mitigate risk from market volatility.

- **Strategic Allocation:** Allocate investments based on long-term value, rarity, and historical significance rather than short-term market trends.

2. Research and Due Diligence

- **Thorough Research:** Conduct extensive research on coins of interest, including their historical background, market trends, and grading standards.

- **Expert Advice:** Consult with numismatic experts, dealers, and grading services to validate authenticity, assess condition, and determine fair market value.

3. Quality Over Quantity

- **Focus on Quality:** Invest in coins with high-grade preservation, strong eye appeal, and provenance that enhances their rarity and market desirability.

- **Long-Term Perspective:** Prioritize coins with enduring collector appeal and potential for appreciation over time, rather than short-term speculative gains.

4. Buy-and-Hold Strategy

- **Patience and Discipline:** Adopt a buy-and-hold strategy for rare coins with strong historical significance and limited supply.

- **Capitalize on Rarity:** Hold coins through market cycles to capitalize on their rarity and historical value, benefiting from potential long-term appreciation.

5. Monitor Market Trends

- **Stay Informed:** Stay updated on numismatic market trends, auction results, and collector preferences through industry publications, online forums, and reputable sources.

- **Adaptability:** Remain flexible in adjusting your investment strategy based on evolving market conditions and emerging opportunities.

Navigating market cycles and implementing effective investment strategies in numismatics requires a blend of knowledge, research, and strategic planning. By understanding market dynamics, diversifying investments, focusing on quality, and maintaining a long-term perspective, collectors and investors can maximize their potential for success in the dynamic world of numismatic investments. Balancing risk and reward while staying informed and adaptable ensures that numismatic investments contribute to both financial growth and the enjoyment of building a valuable coin collection.

Chapter 4: Global perspectives on coin collecting.

Coin collecting, or numismatics, is a hobby and investment pursuit with a rich global history and diverse perspectives. Across different regions and cultures, coin collecting is shaped by unique traditions, historical contexts, market dynamics, and collector motivations. Here's an exploration of global perspectives on coin collecting:

Cultural and Historical Significance

1. Historical Heritage

- **Europe:** In Europe, coin collecting has deep roots dating back to ancient civilizations like Greece and Rome. Medieval and Renaissance periods saw the emergence of coinage as a medium of artistic and political expression, influencing European collectors' fascination with historical coins.

- **Asia:** Countries like China and India have long numismatic traditions, with ancient coins reflecting dynastic eras and cultural milestones. Collectors in Asia often value coins for their historical significance and artistic merit, reflecting broader cultural heritage.

- **Middle East:** Islamic coinage from the Middle East carries religious and historical importance, reflecting the spread of Islam and regional dynasties. Collectors in this region often focus on coins that highlight Islamic art and calligraphy.

2. Colonial and Global Influences

- **Americas:** In the Americas, coin collecting encompasses diverse influences from indigenous cultures, colonial histories, and modern numismatic trends. Collectors may focus on colonial-era coins, modern commemoratives, or indigenous currency systems.

- **Africa:** Numismatics in Africa reflects a blend of indigenous traditions, colonial histories, and modern economic developments. Collectors may seek coins that showcase local cultures, colonial influences, or independence movements.

Market Dynamics and Collector Motivations

1. Investment and Speculation

- **Global Markets:** Numismatic markets worldwide attract collectors and investors seeking tangible assets with historical value and potential for appreciation. Auction houses, online platforms, and numismatic events serve as hubs for buying, selling, and trading coins globally.

- **Emerging Economies:** In emerging economies, rising affluence and cultural appreciation for history drive interest in coin collecting as both a hobby and investment. Collectors may focus on local coinage, foreign rarities, or thematic collections.

2. Cultural Preservation

- **Heritage Preservation:** Numismatics plays a role in preserving cultural heritage by documenting historical events, societal changes, and artistic expressions through coins. Museums and institutions worldwide curate collections that educate and inspire future generations.

3. Educational and Community Engagement

- **Numismatic Education:** Organizations and clubs promote numismatic education through exhibitions, publications, and outreach programs. Educational initiatives foster community engagement and cultivate interest among collectors of all ages.

Technological Advancements and Digital Influence

- **Digital Platforms:** Online databases, mobile apps, and virtual exhibitions enhance accessibility to numismatic information, market trends, and collector communities globally. Digital tools facilitate research, authentication, and networking among collectors worldwide.

Coin collecting transcends geographical boundaries, offering a universal appreciation for history, artistry, and cultural heritage. Global perspectives on coin collecting highlight diverse traditions, market dynamics, and collector motivations that enrich the numismatic community. Whether driven by historical curiosity, investment strategy, or cultural preservation, collectors worldwide contribute to the vibrant and evolving landscape of numismatics. Embracing global perspectives fosters collaboration, knowledge exchange, and mutual appreciation among collectors who share a passion for coins as tangible links to the past and cultural treasures of humanity.

BOOK 10

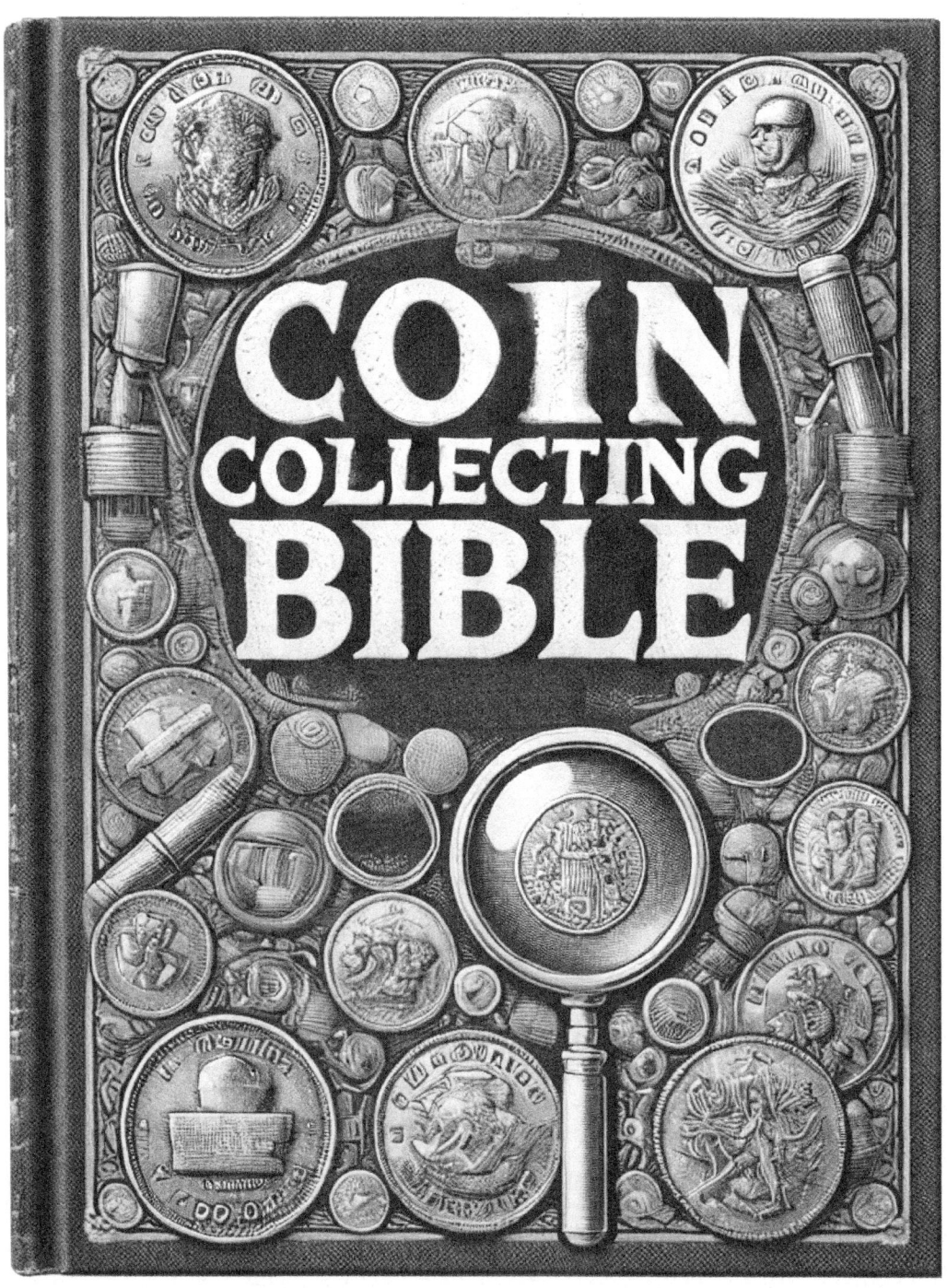

Chapter 1: Ethics and Legal Considerations in Coin Collecting

Coin collecting, like any hobby involving historical artifacts, is subject to a range of ethical considerations and legal regulations aimed at preserving cultural heritage, preventing illicit trade, and ensuring fair practices within the numismatic community. Here's an overview of the key ethics and legal aspects governing coin collecting:

1. Cultural Heritage Protection

- **National Patrimony Laws:** Many countries have laws that designate certain coins or entire categories of cultural artifacts as national treasures. These laws aim to protect items of significant historical or cultural importance from being exported or sold illegally.

- **Archaeological Finds:** Coins discovered through archaeological excavations often fall under strict regulations governing their ownership, excavation, and export. Countries may require permits or licenses for excavations to ensure proper documentation and preservation of cultural context.

2. Ethical Collecting Practices

- **Provenance and Documentation:** Ethical collectors prioritize acquiring coins with documented provenance, ensuring transparency about the coin's history and legal acquisition.

- **Responsible Sourcing:** Collectors should avoid purchasing coins that are suspected of being looted or illegally excavated. They should support reputable dealers and auction houses that adhere to ethical sourcing practices.

3. Legal Frameworks

- **Export and Import Regulations:** International laws regulate the export and import of cultural artifacts, including coins. Collectors need to be aware of these regulations to avoid legal repercussions when acquiring or transporting coins across borders.

- **Ownership and Sales:** Laws vary regarding the ownership and sale of coins, particularly those deemed national treasures or protected under cultural heritage laws. Collectors should understand local regulations to ensure compliance.

4. Numismatic Licensing and Certification

- **Grading and Certification Services:** Coins certified by reputable grading services provide assurance of authenticity and condition. Collectors should verify the credentials of grading services to ensure reliability in the marketplace.

- **Professional Ethics:** Numismatic organizations and associations often establish codes of ethics that guide members in conducting fair and ethical practices, promoting integrity and professionalism in the numismatic community.

5. Collaboration with Authorities

- **Cultural Institutions:** Collaboration between collectors, dealers, and cultural institutions fosters responsible stewardship of numismatic artifacts. This includes donations, loans for exhibitions, and cooperation in research and preservation efforts.

6. Ethical Responsibilities

- **Education and Outreach:** Promoting numismatic education and ethical awareness within the community encourages responsible collecting practices and respect for cultural heritage.

- **Due Diligence:** Conducting thorough research and due diligence before acquiring coins ensures compliance with legal requirements and ethical standards, safeguarding both the collector's reputation and the integrity of the hobby.

Chapter 2: Cultural and Historical Context of Coins

Coins are not just pieces of metal; they are tangible artifacts that embody historical narratives, cultural values, and economic systems throughout human history. Understanding their significance within cultural and historical contexts provides insights into civilizations, trade networks, and societal developments.

Coins as Artifacts of History

- **Symbolism and Iconography:** Coins often bear images of rulers, gods, or significant symbols that reflect the political, religious, and cultural beliefs of their time. For example, ancient Greek coins depicted deities and mythological figures, while Roman coins featured emperors and military victories.

- **Chronology and Dating:** Numismatists use coins as key tools for dating archaeological sites and establishing chronologies. Coins with clear dates or rulers' names provide valuable historical markers, aiding in the interpretation of archaeological finds.

- **Propaganda and Ideology:** Rulers used coinage as a means of propaganda, disseminating their achievements, legitimacy, and political messages to a widespread audience. Coins served as mediums for asserting power and authority over vast territories.

Coins in Archaeological Contexts

- **Stratigraphy and Dating:** Coins found in archaeological excavations help archaeologists establish stratigraphic layers and dating sequences. The presence of coins in specific contexts can reveal trade routes, economic interactions, and cultural exchanges.

- **Hoards and Treasures:** Discoveries of coin hoards, buried for safekeeping or during times of upheaval, provide valuable insights into economic conditions, circulation patterns, and responses to political crises in ancient societies.

- **Material Culture and Daily Life:** Coins offer glimpses into everyday life, revealing what goods were traded, wages paid, and taxes levied. They provide evidence of economic activities, market integration, and social hierarchies within ancient communities.

Monetary Systems and Economic History

- **Development of Coinage:** The invention of coinage marked a significant milestone in economic history, facilitating standardized exchange and trade across regions. Early coins were often made from precious metals like gold, silver, and bronze, reflecting their intrinsic value.

- **Monetary Policies:** Coins reflect shifts in monetary policies, such as debasement (reducing precious metal content) or revaluation efforts by rulers to stabilize economies or fund military campaigns.

- **Trade and Commerce:** Coins played a pivotal role in fostering trade networks and commercial expansion. They enabled merchants to conduct transactions efficiently and contributed to the integration of distant markets in ancient times.

Ethical collecting practices

Ethical collecting practices in numismatics are essential for preserving cultural heritage, promoting responsible stewardship of historical artifacts, and ensuring integrity within the numismatic community. Here are key principles and guidelines that guide ethical coin collecting:

Chapter 3: Principles of Ethical Collecting Practices

1. Respect for Cultural Heritage

- **Legal Compliance:** Adhere to national and international laws governing the acquisition, ownership, and export of cultural artifacts, including coins. Respect regulations aimed at preserving archaeological sites and national patrimony.

- **Avoidance of Illicit Trade:** Refrain from acquiring coins that are suspected of being looted, illegally excavated, or trafficked. Support efforts to combat the illicit trade of cultural property and promote ethical sourcing practices.

2. Documentation and Provenance

- **Documented History:** Prefer coins with clear provenance and documented history of ownership. Transparent documentation helps verify authenticity, legality of acquisition, and historical context.

- **Due Diligence:** Conduct thorough research on the background of coins before acquisition. Verify authenticity through reputable dealers, auction houses, or certified grading services.

3. Responsible Collecting Practices

- **Conservation and Preservation:** Handle coins with care to avoid damage and deterioration. Use appropriate storage methods and materials that ensure long-term preservation without altering the coin's integrity or patina.

- **Support Conservation Efforts:** Contribute to efforts aimed at preserving cultural heritage, such as donations to museums, participation in archaeological projects, or funding research in numismatics.

4. Ethical Selling and Trading

- **Full Disclosure:** Provide accurate and complete information about coins when selling or trading. Disclose any restoration, alteration, or significant characteristics that may affect the coin's value or authenticity.

- **Fair Market Practices:** Conduct transactions with honesty, fairness, and respect for the rights of buyers and sellers. Avoid misleading or deceptive practices that undermine trust within the numismatic community.

5. Educational Outreach

- **Promote Numismatic Education:** Share knowledge and resources with fellow collectors, scholars, and the public. Educate others about the historical significance, artistic value, and cultural context of numismatic artifacts.

- **Ethical Mentorship:** Mentor new collectors and encourage ethical collecting practices. Foster a community of integrity and mutual respect among numismatists through ethical leadership and guidance.

Challenges and Considerations

- **Repatriation and Cultural Sensitivity:** Respect cultural sensitivities and support efforts for the repatriation of cultural property to its country of origin when appropriate.

- **Emerging Issues:** Stay informed about emerging ethical challenges in numismatics, such as digital replicas, counterfeiting, and the impact of online markets on cultural heritage preservation.

Ethical collecting practices uphold the values of integrity, respect for cultural heritage, and responsible stewardship within the numismatic community. By adhering to ethical guidelines, collectors contribute to the preservation and appreciation of historical artifacts, ensuring that coins continue to serve as valuable links to our shared human history. Embracing ethical principles fosters trust, sustainability, and the enduring legacy of numismatics as a respected field of study and enjoyment.

Conclusion

In conclusion, "The Coin Collecting Bible" serves as a comprehensive guide and companion for enthusiasts of all levels embarking on the rewarding journey of numismatics. Throughout this book, we've explored the rich tapestry of coin collecting, delving into its historical, cultural, and economic significance across civilizations and continents.

From the ancient coins of Greece and Rome to the intricacies of modern numismatic markets, this book has navigated the evolution of coinage, the artistry of design, and the methodologies of preservation and valuation. We've examined ethical considerations, legal frameworks, and the importance of responsible collecting practices in safeguarding cultural heritage.

Moreover, "The Coin Collecting Bible" has celebrated the passion and diversity within the numismatic community, highlighting the global perspectives that enrich our understanding of coins as more than mere currency—they are tangible connections to our shared human story.

As you embark on your own numismatic journey, may this book serve as a trusted resource, offering insights, guidance, and inspiration to explore, appreciate, and preserve the fascinating world of coin collecting. Whether you collect for historical curiosity, investment opportunities, or the sheer joy of discovery, may your numismatic pursuits be guided by curiosity, integrity, and a deep appreciation for the enduring legacy of coins.

Thank you for joining me on this exploration of "The Coin Collecting Bible." May your collection continue to grow and evolve, reflecting the breadth and beauty of numismatic treasures found throughout the ages.

BONUSES

BONUS 1 – DETAILED COIN CLEANING AND PRESERVATION GUIDE

BONUS 2 – LIST OF BETTER DIGITAL COINVALUATION TOOLS

BONUS 3 - COLLECTORS CHECKLIST LINK

Printed in Great Britain
by Amazon

54597461R00090